COMIC BOOK CENTURY

JUST AS EACH GENERATION

WRITES ITS OWN HISTORY, EACH

READS ITS OWN COMIC BOOKS.

—BRADFORD W. WRIGHT,
WRITER AND HISTORIAN

COMIC BOOK CENTURY

THE HISTORY OF AMERICAN COMIC BOOKS

Stephen Krensky

TFCB

TWENTY-FIRST CENTURY BOOKS · MINNEAPOLIS

Twenty-First Century Books
A division of Lerner Publishing Group, Inc.
241 First Avenue North
Minneapolis, MN 55401 U.S.A.

Website address: www.lernerbooks.com

Library of Congress Cataloging-in-Publication Data

Krensky, Stephen.
    Comic book century : the history of American comic books / by Stephen Krensky.
        p.   cm. — (People's history)
    Includes bibliographical references and index.
    ISBN-13: 978–0–8225–6654–0 (lib. bdg. : alk. paper)
    ISBN-10: 0–8225–6654–0 (lib. bdg. : alk. paper)
    1. Comic books, strips, etc.—United States—History and criticism.
    I. Title.
    PN6725.K74 2008
    741.5'9730904—dc22   2006020795

Manufactured in the United States of America
2 3 4 5 6 7 – BP – 13 12 11 10 09 08

CONTENTS

INTRODUCTION

I'M GOING TO BE A BOY SCOUT. IT MUST BE GREAT. I'M GOING TO BE A BOY SCOUT RIGHT NOW.
I'M GOING TO BE A DOG SCOUT
AM I TOO LATE TO JOIN ?
NO
JOIN NOW
BOY SCOUT

Buster Brown and his dog, Tige *(above)*, first appeared in 1902 in a *New York Herald* comic strip. Created by Richard F. Outcault, *Buster Brown* remained popular for decades.

See ya in the funny papers.

—slang phrase from the 1920s and 1930s

Popular culture—movies, music, best-selling novels—has always had two sides. On the one hand, it mirrors the interests and opinions of society. On the other, it often helps to change society by spreading ideas and feelings. The influence of comic books in American society is no exception. They first became very popular in the 1930s—the era of the Great Depression—and from the beginning, they have influenced our fears, our desires, and our attitudes.

The Great Depression was a difficult time in the United States, as it was across the world. In October 1929, the U.S. stock market crashed as investors panicked over the falling value of their stocks. An economic crisis followed the crash. Investors lost their fortunes, and banks across the country closed. Unable to keep their businesses and factories open, many owners were forced to fire their employees. The unemployed could not afford to buy goods or services, so more businesses closed and more employees lost their jobs. By 1933 one in four American workers was unemployed. Workers and farmers who once owned their own homes and lived comfortably became dependent on charity. They stood in bread lines for food, wore secondhand clothing, and took odd jobs just to earn a few cents.

For many people, the economic depression caused emotional depression. Even those who managed to keep their jobs through the 1930s worried daily about the future. So Americans looked to books, music, and movies to forget their troubles for a little while. Some popular media soothed the trauma of poverty and helplessness. Novels such as John Steinbeck's *The Grapes of Wrath* or songs such as "Brother, Can You Spare a Dime?" urged society to treat ordinary, hardworking people fairly. Other popular media were pure entertainment. For

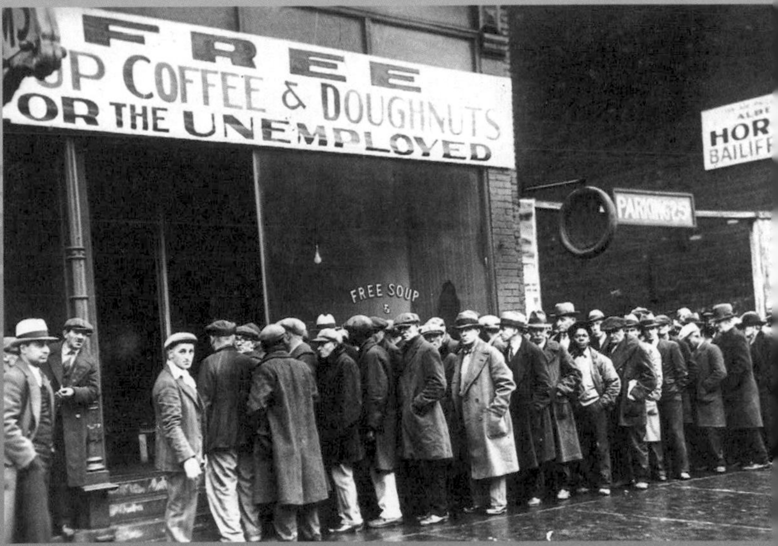
FREE
COFFEE & DOUGHNUTS
THE UNEMPLOYED
FREE SOUP
PARKING

Jobless people in the 1930s wait in line for free coffee and doughnuts. "Bread lines" like this one were common in the United States during the Great Depression.

fifteen cents a ticket, movies such as *Duck Soup* and *My Man Godfrey* provided fast-paced comedy, while *Gunga Din* and *Footlight Parade* thrilled audiences with exciting adventure and flashy dancing.

Americans also looked for new and different ways to brighten their moods. One new way rose to great popularity in the mid-1930s—the comic book.

Comic Strips Blaze a Trail

American comic books owe their beginnings to newspaper comic strips, which had been published in the United States for decades. The strips—boxed panels filled with illustrations and text—were called the funny papers, or the funnies. They appeared every Sunday, the day most newspapers put out their largest edition. Many people read the funnies before they read anything else. Popular and long-running strips featured humorous best friends Mutt and Jeff, the heroic ape-man Tarzan, and sentimental sweetheart Little Orphan Annie.

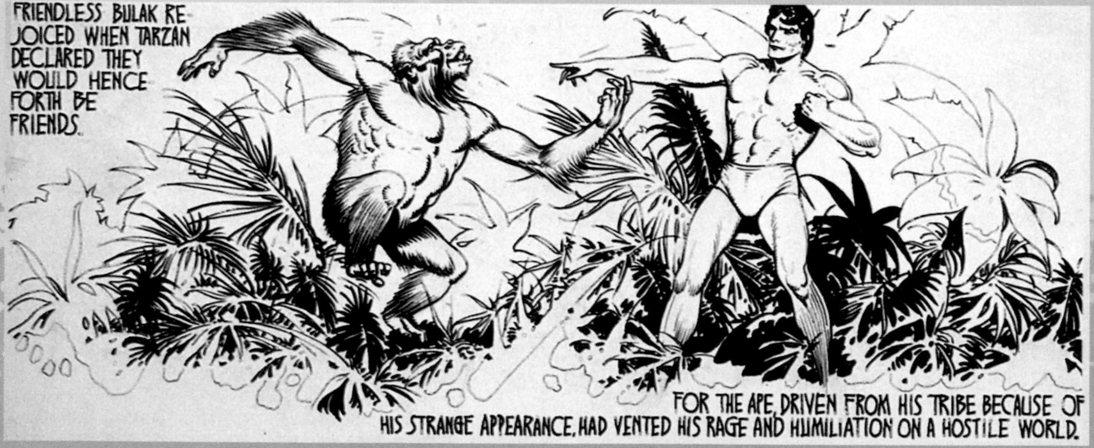
FRIENDLESS BULAK REJOICED WHEN TARZAN DECLARED THEY WOULD HENCEFORTH BE FRIENDS.
FOR THE APE, DRIVEN FROM HIS TRIBE BECAUSE OF HIS STRANGE APPEARANCE, HAD VENTED HIS RAGE AND HUMILIATION ON A HOSTILE WORLD.

Tarzan was a popular 1930s comic strip character. The comic strip was based on *Tarzan of the Apes*, a 1912 novel by Edgar Rice Burroughs. In the novel, Tarzan is a young English boy shipwrecked on an isolated island. He is raised into adulthood by the island's apes.

NO. 9
FAMOUS FUNNIES
The Nation's Comic Monthly
10 CENTS
I JUST COULDN'T BEAR TO WAKE HIM UP!
WET PAINT
In this Issue
BUCK ROGERS
DAN DUNN
JOE PALOOKA
JANE ARDEN
HAIRBREADTH HARRY
NED BRANT
BARNACLE BILL
FLYING TO FAME
NAPOLEON
MESCAL IKE
—and many more
100 COLOR COMICS
April

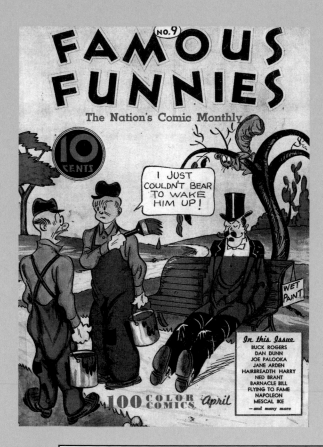

In 1934 the creators of *Famous Funnies* had a hard time convincing their bosses that anyone would pay ten cents for a comic book.

Comic strips proved so popular that a few publishers began gathering published strips and reprinting them in book form. Some of these early comic books were large, others were small. Some were sold at sidewalk newsstands while others were given away as advertising gimmicks. The first comic strip collection published regularly in a standard comic book format was *Famous Funnies* in 1934. Its creators were Max Gaines and Harry Wildenberg, two salesmen who worked for a Connecticut printing company. The books reprinted humor, detective, monster, and adventure comic strips. They were sold at newsstands for ten cents an issue. *Famous Funnies* was not an immediate hit, but Gaines and Wildenberg stuck with it, and the books were soon making a profit.

Also in 1934, New York publisher Dell followed *Famous Funnies* into the comic book business by printing a collection of comic strips called *Popular Comics*. Both these ventures were popular, but it was expensive for publishers to pay for the legal right to reprint famous newspaper strips. Major Malcolm Wheeler-Nicholson knew that it would be cheaper to hire writers and artists to create new, original stories for comic books. And his opinion matters because he gets credit for creating the first original comic book.

The major was a former army officer who for years had been writing military adventure stories for pulp magazines—fiction magazines printed on cheap paper. He had also formed his own company to syndicate comic strips, or sell them to several newspapers across the country. But Wheeler-Nicholson also saw the potential in selling original comic books. So, in late 1934, he founded National Allied Publications. At first, the most impressive thing about the company was its name. There was not much behind it, national or local—no large office, no hardworking staff. Wheeler-Nicholson, however, hoped to change that.

The next year, in 1935, National Allied's first comic book, *New Fun Comics*, appeared. The early issues were seven inches wide by ten inches high and had thirty-two pages. The covers were printed in color, but the strips inside were black and white. *New Fun Comics* was not an immediate success, so Wheeler-Nicholson took another look at his format. He decided to reduce the books' dimensions and to increase the number of pages to eighty. He also began using color inside. By 1937 National Allied Publications was renamed Detective Comics (and later simply DC) for its emphasis on mystery and crime stories.

By the late 1930s, comic books were a booming industry. While newspaper strips were aimed at readers of all ages, original comic books had more specific audiences in mind—especially children. The success of adventure books such as the Hardy Boys series, which featured two teenage brothers solving mysteries, had shown that profits could be made from young readers. Larger, established companies joined the comic book boom, forming King Comics (owned by King Features Syndicate), Tip Top Comics (owned by United Features), and others. The era became known as the Golden Age of Comics.

Readers loved the new comic books. The combination of pictures and text bridged different reading abilities and interests. And the varied stories—Old West adventures, romantic dramas, horror tales, comic animal yarns, and law-and-order hero stories—provided something for everyone. Best of all, comic books were cheap enough that almost everyone could afford to buy them.

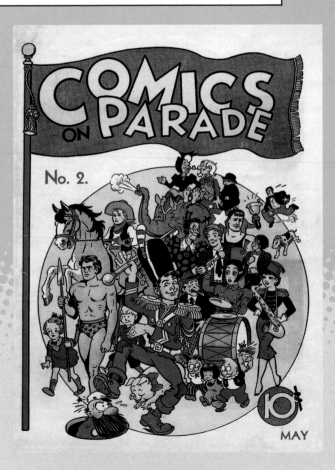

Comics on Parade—a comic book popular in the 1930s—provided readers with a variety of stories and characters.

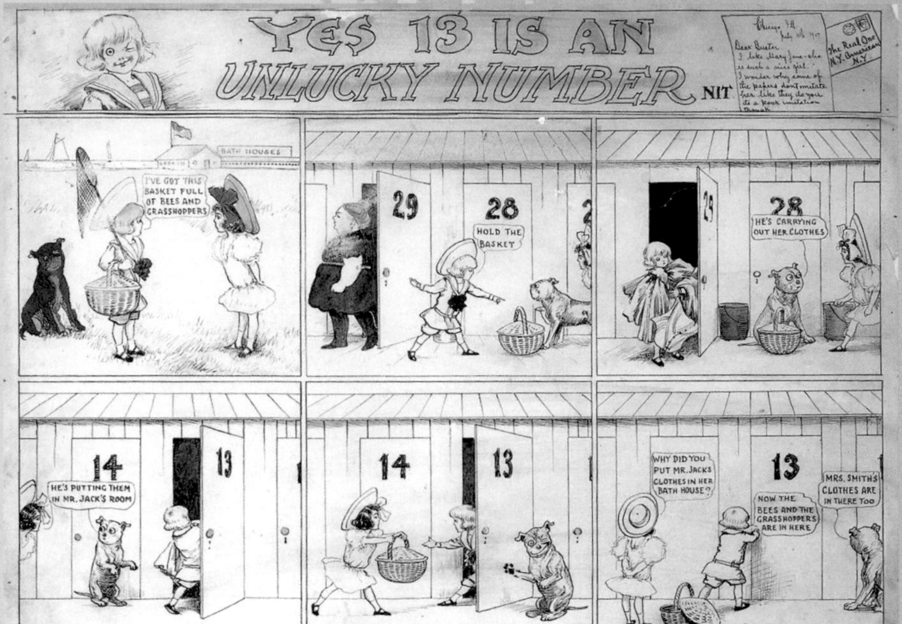
YES 13 IS AN UNLUCKY NUMBER
NIT
Dear Buster
The Real One N.Y. American N.Y.
BATH HOUSES
I'VE GOT THIS BASKET FULL OF BEES AND GRASSHOPPERS
29
28
HOLD THE BASKET
HE'S CARRYING OUT HER CLOTHES
14
13
HE'S PUTTING THEM IN MR. JACK'S ROOM
14
13
WHY DID YOU PUT MR. JACKS CLOTHES IN HER BATH HOUSE?
13
NOW THE BEES AND THE GRASSHOPPERS ARE IN HERE
MRS. SMITH'S CLOTHES ARE IN THERE TOO
29
28
HELP-THERES A MAN'S CLOTHES IN HERE
29
28
HELP
28
I'M IN THE WRONG ROOM
13
SOME ONE'S HURT
WHATS THE MATTER?
RUN QUICK
20
I'M GOING BATHING NOW
RESOLVED
THEY SAID THAT IT WAS CIRCUMSTANTIAL EVIDENCE WHO POINTED TO ME, BECAUSE I DIDN'T RUN WITH THE CROWD - I DONT LIKE CROWDS. CIRCUMSTANTIAL EVIDENCE SHOWS THAT 13 ISN'T UNLUCKY. THERE IS NO SUCH THING AS LUCK. I PUT THOSE BEES IN 13 FOR FUN. WHEN YOU BELIEVE IN LUCK YOU'RE IN A BAD FIX. GOD MADE YOU, BELIEVE IN YOURSELF AND HUSTLE, THEN LUCK, GOOD OR BAD WONT BOTHER YOU. HOW COULD THERE BE ANY SUCH THING AS LUCK? DONT LETS BE PINHEADS, YOU MIGHT AS WELL BELIEVE THERES A SATAN AND A HADES
B. B.
R. F. Outcault

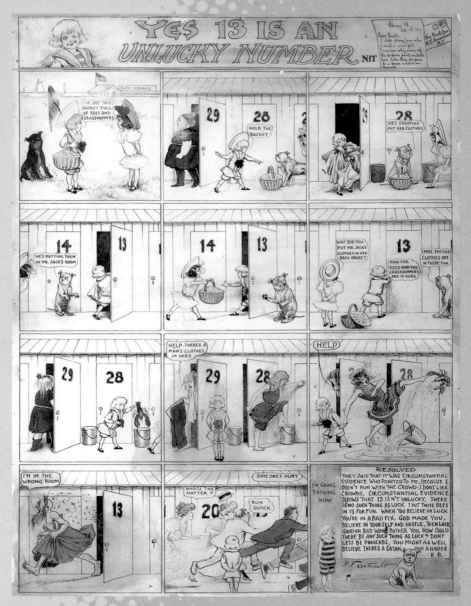

When reading a comic, the action unfolds, panel by panel, from left to right and top to bottom. Creating a readable story with pictures and dialogue is not as easy as it may at first appear. This set of panels is from *Buster Brown*.

TELLING TALES

Comic books may have been cheap to buy, but they were not easy to produce. A comic book page may look straightforward enough. Each page usually has four or five panels, each containing an action or an exchange of dialogue or both. The spaces between panels represent the passage of time. This is simple enough. But each comic book page contains layers of work.

First, a writer creates the characters and action that will take place in the story. The penciller uses the writer's words to make pencil drawings of each scene. Doing this effectively is a balancing act. How much of the story should be presented in words? How much in pictures? How do you keep the pages from getting repetitive?

After the penciling is complete, the inker fills in the pencil lines and shadows with ink. The colorist tints the clothing, skin, eyes, outdoor skies, interior lighting, and every other detail. Then the letterer carefully places narration boxes and dialogue and thought balloons. All these creative talents work together to create the final product, a comic book ready for thousands of fans.

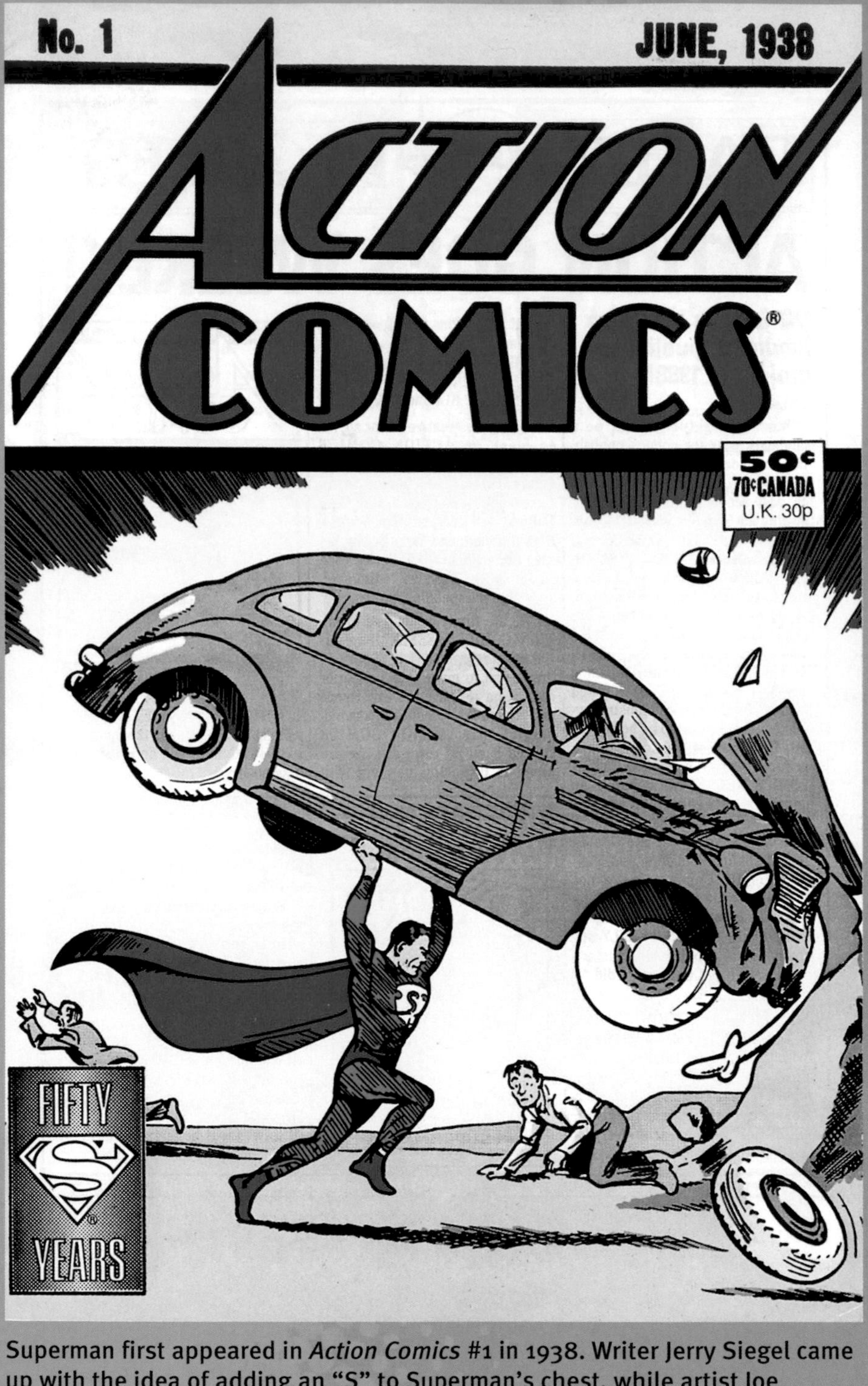
No. 1
JUNE, 1938
ACTION COMICS®
50¢
70¢CANADA
U.K. 30p
FIFTY
YEARS

Superman first appeared in *Action Comics* #1 in 1938. Writer Jerry Siegel came up with the idea of adding an "S" to Superman's chest, while artist Joe Shuster added a cape to convey the idea of motion, especially flying. Both the "S" and the cape became famous symbols of the superhero.

SUPERHEROES TAKE OFF

> **Early, Clark decided he must turn his titanic strength into channels that would benefit mankind. And so was created . . . Superman!**
>
> *—Jerry Siegel,*
> Action Comics *#1, 1938*

No master plan guided the evolution of American comic books from newspaper strip collections to their own art form. Nobody sat around an office deciding who should come first and what should happen next. Publishers tried out all kinds of characters or story lines. If they sold, the publishers stuck with them. If they did not sell, the publishers tried something else.

One type of character—the superhero— struck a chord with depression-era comic book readers and quickly became a staple of the industry. Superheroes are characters possessed of supernatural powers or extraordinary human strengths. They generally use these abilities to fight injustice and defend the weak.

Heroes, of course, were not new to popular literature. They could trace their heritage to ancient times, to Greek and Norse myths, for example. Some heroes had great strength or other special powers. Or, like Robin Hood, they might defeat villains with wit and skill.

Heroes with secret identities also had a long tradition in popular literature. In 1905 Hungarian-English author Emmuska Orczy published *The Scarlet Pimpernel,* a novel about a masked hero who rescues French aristocrats from execution during the French

Douglas Fairbanks played Zorro (wearing mask) in a series of movies in the 1920s. Handsome and athletic, Fairbanks was one of Hollywood's first action heroes. He made a career of playing pirates, cowboys, detectives, and heroes from literature.

Revolution (1789–1799). Without his mask, the Pimpernel is a supposedly timid English lord named Sir Percy Blakeney. In 1919 Johnston McCulley also used the theme of the hero with a secret identity in *The Curse of Capistrano*. Set in Spanish California in the early nineteenth century, the novel features a masked figure named Zorro. An expert horseback rider and swordsman, Zorro swoops in to defend the poor against a harsh and corrupt government. Zorro keeps his identity secret by appearing in public as Don Diego de la Vega, a weak and cowardly Spanish nobleman.

The heirs to these mysterious fictional heroes found their way into the daily comic strips and radio programs of the 1930s. Prominent among them was the Phantom, a popular radio-era hero created by writer Lee Falk. The first Phantom was a sailor who shipwrecked off the coast of Africa. A local Pygmy tribe restored his health. After his recovery, the Phantom took an oath, swearing to fight piracy, greed, cruelty, and injustice. The Phantom has no superpowers, but he is the twenty-first in a line of heroic crime-fighting family members. Each Phantom has worn the same costume—a purple body suit, striped trunks, and black mask—and so the legend grows of the first Phantom living on through the centuries. Seemingly immortal, the Phantom becomes known as the Ghost Who Walks.

Other superheroes followed in the Phantom's footsteps. One of these became the first great comic book superhero of the 1930s and would go on to become one of the most famous figures in pop culture. The man of steel—a towering symbol of truth, justice, and the American way—had his start in the mind of two shy young men.

Look! Up in the Sky!

"As a high school student," Jerry Siegel remembered, "I thought that someday I might become a reporter, and I had crushes on several attractive girls who either didn't know I existed or didn't care I existed. So it occurred to me: What if I was really terrific? What if I had something special going for me, like jumping over buildings or throwing cars around or something like that?"

These youthful musings led to the creation of Superman. Siegel and his friend Joe Shuster attended high school in Cleveland, Ohio. They were both science fiction fans. They also thrilled to the exploits of the jungle man Tarzan (who by the 1930s had become a popular comic-strip star) and to the adventures of movie heroes such as Douglas Fairbanks. After high school, in the early 1930s, the friends began discussing the idea of a character named Superman. Siegel even published a science fiction story, "The Reign of Superman," in 1933. The early version of the character is a villain. He has special mental powers, but he uses them to further his own evil purposes.

In a 1983 interview, Siegel recalled how the character developed after that. "A couple of months after I published this story, it occurred to me that a Superman as a hero rather than as a villain might make a great comic strip character. . . ." Siegel imagined Superman as a hero along the lines of Tarzan but with more extraordinary powers.

Like the Scarlet Pimpernel, Zorro, and the Phantom, Superman came with a secret identity. When not leaping over tall buildings, Superman was a timid newspaper reporter, Clark Kent. Siegel recalled that Clark's character was taken from his own experiences. "The concept came to me that Superman could have a dual identity, and that in one of his identities he could be meek and mild, as I was, and wear glasses, the way I do." Clark Kent is in love with Lois Lane, another reporter at the *Daily Star* (later the *Daily Planet*). But Lois

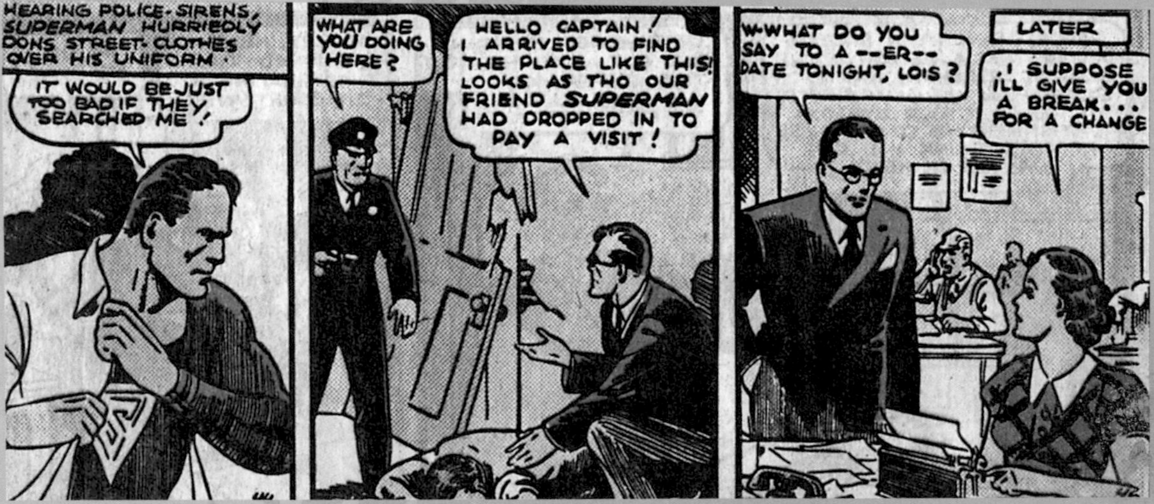
HEARING POLICE-SIRENS, SUPERMAN HURRIEDLY DONS STREET-CLOTHES OVER HIS UNIFORM.
IT WOULD BE JUST TOO BAD IF THEY SEARCHED ME!
WHAT ARE YOU DOING HERE?
HELLO CAPTAIN! I ARRIVED TO FIND THE PLACE LIKE THIS! LOOKS AS THO OUR FRIEND SUPERMAN HAD DROPPED IN TO PAY A VISIT!
W-WHAT DO YOU SAY TO A --ER-- DATE TONIGHT, LOIS?
LATER
..I SUPPOSE I'LL GIVE YOU A BREAK... FOR A CHANGE

When not in uniform as Superman, Clark Kent is a shy, bespectacled newspaper reporter. He has no luck in his romantic pursuit of fellow reporter Lois Lane.

does not return Clark's feelings. In fact, in an ironic twist, Lois is madly in love with Superman.

In the mid-1930s, Siegel and Shuster got jobs at DC (then called DC-National). They worked as a team, with Siegel writing adventure and crime-fighting comic book stories and Shuster illustrating them. They tried several times, with no success, to convince DC to publish Superman stories. But as their reputations as a writer and an illustrator grew, DC took their proposal more seriously. Finally, Superman made his debut in *Action Comics #1* in 1938. In that first issue, Superman came from an unnamed distant planet. He showed extraordinary powers. He could leap great distances, he had super strength, and his eyes gave him heat vision, X-ray vision, and telescopic vision.

After a few months, Superman's popularity erupted. At that time, a successful comic book might sell one hundred thousand copies for each issue, but Superman was soon selling more than one million.

As the series continued, readers learned that Superman was the last survivor of the planet Krypton. Before Krypton exploded, the infant Superman's parents Jor-El and Lara sent him to Earth in a small spaceship. The spaceship crashed in a field in Smallville, Kansas. Farmers Jonathan and Martha Kent found the ship with the healthy baby inside. They adopted the baby and named him Clark. The Kents soon discovered that young Clark was full of surprises. As Clark set out on his career as a hero, he amazed his readers too.

What made Superman such a success with his readers? Among various factors, his many powers were exciting to fantasize about. And he used those powers to do good deeds, to battle crime and injustice. By the late 1930s, the grip of the Great Depression was easing and people were doing a little better economically. But there were other growing social problems and political threats. Daniele Di Piazza, a retired political science professor from Wisconsin, was an avid comic book fan as a boy in the 1930s. He recalls, "It was a time of lots of crime and the rise of Fascism [a violent extremist political movement gaining power in Europe]. These dangers seemed to have been reflected in many comics—hence the clear definition of good guys and bad guys. There was the need for special powers to fight these evils, which is why there were comic book heroes with extra or super powers." The idea of Superman making the world a better place gave people a sense of hope about the future.

Not only was Superman popular (he was the first hero ever to get his own comic book), he soon became the subject of a newspaper comic strip and a radio program. The radio program introduced the famous phrases describing Superman's prowess: "faster than a speeding bullet" and "more powerful than a locomotive." And it included the famous lines: "Look! Up in the sky! It's a bird! It's a plane! It's Superman!"

Enter the Bat

Other publishers were eager to grab onto Superman's cape and share in his success. But readers were not looking for pale imitations of Superman. They hoped for something more. Such a figure first appeared in DC's *Detective Comics* #27 in 1939. He was Batman, the Caped Crusader. Batman is a super detective. Superman might arrive to save the day and catch villains in the act. But Batman wanders the city by night, trying to figure things out in advance.

Batman needed that extra edge. He was a costumed crime fighter, but he had no super physical powers. Batman's alter ego is Bruce Wayne, a wealthy businessman. To transform into Batman, Wayne simply dons the Bat costume. But Wayne—and Batman—is smart, acrobatic, an expert at the martial arts, and a scientific wizard who invents all kinds of amazing gadgets.

Batman was the creation of artist Bob Kane. Kane was twenty-three years old when Batman was first published. His inspiration came from many sources. "I remember," Kane said in an interview, "when I was twelve or thirteen, I was an ardent reader of books on how things began—the automobile, the steam engine, the para-chute—and I came across a book about Leonardo da Vinci. This had

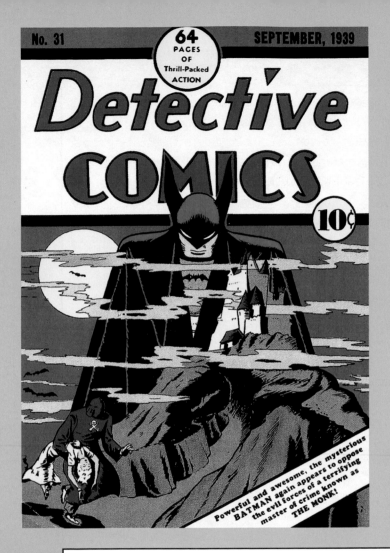

No. 31 — **64 PAGES OF Thrill-Packed ACTION** — SEPTEMBER, 1939

Detective **COMICS** 10¢

Powerful and awesome, the mysterious BATMAN again appears to oppose the evil forces of a terrifying master of crime known as THE MONK!

Batman flew onto the superhero scene in 1939 as a character in *Detective Comics.*

a picture of a flying machine with huge bat wings. . . . It looked like a bat man to me." He also recalled a movie from his childhood called *The Bat,* which featured a villain in a batlike costume.

Like Superman, Batman has a tragic personal history. As a young boy, Bruce Wayne had watched a robber gun down his parents. Years later, he became Batman to avenge his parents' death.

And why a bat? The comic book itself explains what happened. Wayne is sitting in his study wondering what shape his costume should take. "Criminals are a superstitious cowardly lot. So my disguise must be able to strike terror into their hearts. I must be a creature of the night, a black, terrible..." The next panel shows a bat flying in the open window. "A bat!" Wayne exclaims. "That's it! It's an omen. I shall become a bat!"

Batman is a darker hero than Superman. While Superman faces his share of dastardly villains, he faces them rather cheerfully. He also tries to make sure they do not get hurt while he brings them to justice. Batman has no such concerns. In his first adventure, the villain falls into a vat of acid. And what is Batman's comment? "A fitting end for his kind."

Kane's first writing partner was Bill Finger, who developed the story for much of Batman's personal background. He saw Batman as an athletic Sherlock Holmes—nineteenth-century novelist Arthur Conan Doyle's famous fictional detective from London, England. As Batman

Writer Bill Finger compared Batman to Sherlock Holmes, the super-smart fictional detective. In 1939, the same year *Batman* was launched, Sherlock Holmes became a movie star. British actor Basil Rathbone *(left)* starred as Holmes in *The Hound of the Baskervilles*, the first in a popular series of Sherlock Holmes films.

worked through the twists and turns in the plots, Kane and Finger had to find a way to explain to readers what Batman was thinking. At first, Batman spent a lot of time talking to himself as a way of also talking to the reader. But Kane and Finger decided that Batman really needed someone else around. In Sherlock Holmes stories, Holmes explains his thoughts to his friend Dr. Watson. Kane and Finger decided to create a companion for Batman too. And so appeared Robin, the Boy Wonder, in the spring of 1939.

Robin was originally Dick Grayson, whose family were circus trapeze artists. Dick's parents are killed in a supposed accident arranged by gangsters trying to muscle in on the circus. After their deaths, Bruce Wayne adopts the boy. The Caped Crusader now had himself a sidekick.

As Superman and Batman's popularity grew, other superheroes appeared in comics. The Sub-Mariner and the Human Torch, for example, were both created in 1939. And by the end of the 1930s, the United States was in need of heroes. The anxiety and hardship of the Great Depression was easing. But threats of another kind of disaster loomed large. Germany's Nazi Party, led by dictator Adolf Hitler, sought to dominate Europe. With Italy and Japan, Germany formed the Axis powers with the intent to invade and take over other countries in Europe and Asia. To fight against them, Great Britain, France, and several other smaller countries formed the Allied powers. By 1939 World War II had begun in Europe.

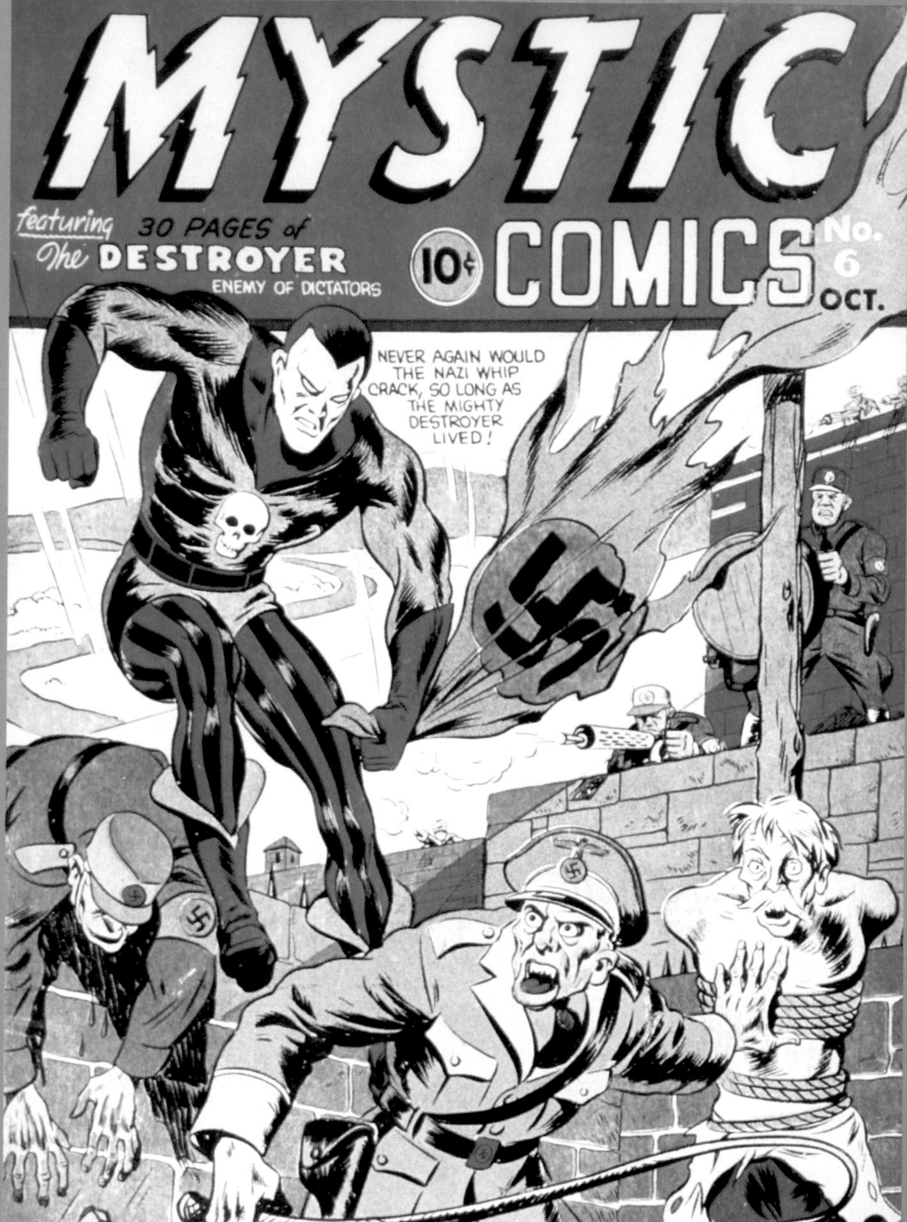
MYSTIC
featuring 30 PAGES of
The DESTROYER
ENEMY OF DICTATORS
10¢
COMICS
No. 6
OCT.
NEVER AGAIN WOULD THE NAZI WHIP CRACK, SO LONG AS THE MIGHTY DESTROYER LIVED!

Before he became a superhero, the Destroyer was Keen Marlowe, an American newspaper reporter. Arrested by the Nazis in Germany, Marlowe is sent to a prison camp, where he befriends a German scientist working against the Nazis. The scientist gives Marlowe a secret formula that transforms the reporter into a super-soldier. After escaping prison, Marlowe dons his Destroyer disguise and vows to crush the Nazis.

THE COMICS GO TO WAR

Never again would the Nazi whip crack, so long as the mighty Destroyer lived!

—*Mystic Comics #6, October 1941*

Hitler's Nazi war machine was strong, and it swept quickly across western Europe. Holland, Belgium, and France fell. By the summer of 1940, Great Britain was the only Allied power still actively battling the Nazis. German planes regularly bombed England's railroads, airports, and factories in an effort to cripple the British military. The Nazis also bombed residential areas in London and other parts of the British Isles, hoping to force the British people to give up. But the killing of civilians only outraged the British, and they refused to surrender.

For a time, the United States remained formally neutral, not having declared war on any country. After the bombing of Great Britain, U.S. president Franklin D. Roosevelt and many Americans believed the United States should end the neutrality and join the Allies. U.S. military forces, in fact, had started to prepare for fighting overseas. But other Americans believed the United States should stay out of the war. Whether the country *could* remain neutral, however, was a growing question. The United States had every reason to fear that Germany's ally Japan would attack from the west, targeting Hawaii, California, and other parts of the U.S. Pacific Coast.

The comic book world by this time was filled with superheroes.

Superman and Batman were not alone. Captain Marvel, the Destroyer, the Human Torch, the Sub-Mariner, the Green Lantern, the Spectre, and others had all found a ready audience. Captain Marvel, in fact, became comics' most popular superhero—more popular than Superman and Batman—after he first appeared in Fawcett comic books in 1940.

Like Superman and Batman, Captain Marvel has a secret identity. He is actually a teenager named Billy Batson. Billy is a poor orphan whose uncle had stolen his inheritance after the death of his parents. Billy is barely making a living selling newspapers and ends up sleeping near the entrance to a subway station. One day a mysterious figure asks Billy to follow him down into the subway. A special train carries them to a secret hideaway. There the figure reveals himself as a powerful wizard who has chosen Billy to be Earth's champion.

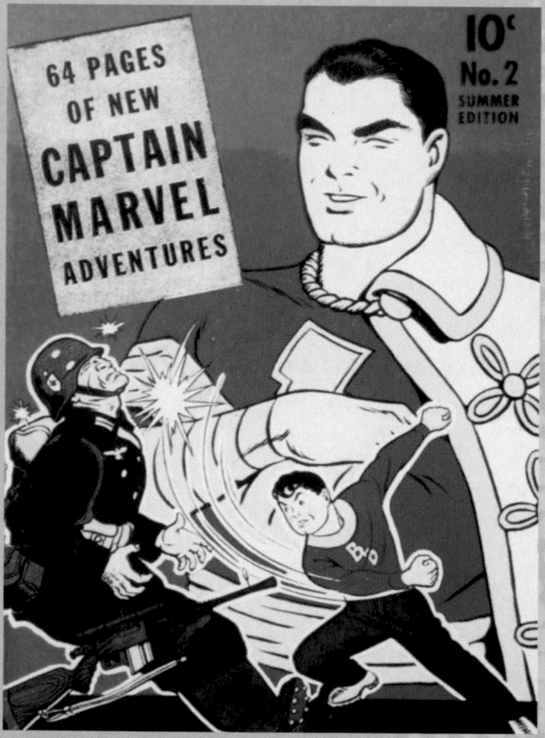
64 PAGES OF NEW
CAPTAIN MARVEL
ADVENTURES
10¢
No. 2
SUMMER EDITION

Captain Marvel was the most popular superhero in U.S. comics during World War II (1939–1945). In 1941 he also became the first comics superhero to get his own movie deal—a twelve-part serial for Republic Pictures.

But Billy is not going to do this without help. The wizard instructs him to say the magic word *SHAZAM*. When he does, he turns into the World's Mightiest Mortal. SHAZAM gives Billy the special powers of several figures from biblical and ancient mythology—the wisdom of *S*olomon, the strength of *H*ercules, the stamina of *A*tlas, the power of *Z*eus, the courage of *A*chilles, and the speed of *M*ercury.

Young readers liked Captain Marvel because they could identify with his origins as an ordinary kid. But not everyone was thrilled that children were reading more and more comics. In a 1940 editorial published in the *Chicago Daily News*, book reviewer Sterling North criticized comic books as "pulp-paper nightmares." North wrote, "Badly drawn, badly written, and badly printed—a strain on the young eyes and young nervous systems. . . . Unless we want a coming generation even more ferocious than the present one, parents and teachers throughout America must band together to break the 'comic' magazine."

Despite such criticism, superheroes were as popular as ever. But their battles with street thugs, gangsters, and otherworldly villains began to seem irrelevant in the shadow of a world war.

A Hero for the Time

One of DC's main competitors was about to help comic books join the real world. Timely Comics published many different comics, including a series with the same word in every title: Marvel Science Stories, Marvel Tales, and, finally, Marvel Comics. (None of these had anything to do with Captain Marvel. The company simply knew a good word when it heard it.) Timely's publisher was Martin Goodman, and for him, the threat of world war was more than an event to provide material for a new commercial trend. It was a cause worth fighting for.

Goodman was already publishing two well-known superheroes, the Human Torch and the Sub-Mariner. The Human Torch, conceived by Carl Burgos, is not really human at all. He is an android—a humanlike robot—created in a lab. The Human Torch escapes the lab by accident and in time becomes a crime fighter. Prince Namor, the Sub-Mariner, was the work of Bill Everett. The prince is a half-human mer-man with a big chip on his shoulder because he does not like what the land-loving humans are doing to his planet—especially the ocean.

As the war continued in Europe, Timely's heroes jumped in. Both the Sub-Mariner and the Human Torch began taking on real-life bad guys—in this case, the Nazis. While Americans worried about who would win the battles overseas, readers knew there was no contest about who would win the comic book fights.

The most famous patriotic hero of the era was Captain America. He was the creation of Jack Kirby and Joe Simon. Born Jacob Kurtzberg in 1917, Kirby had grown up in a poor area of New York City. He had started his drawing career in 1935 and by 1937 was drawing comic strips. At that time, twenty-two-year-old Joe Simon was a sports illustrator for a Syracuse, New York, newspaper. When they met and started working together, they made a good team.

The new comic book duo brought a heightened sense of visual action to their comics. Their tightly connected panels varied in size, a visual change from the uniform newspaper comic strip panels of the day.

"The usual practice," Simon recalls, "was that I would do the writing right on the page in pencil, in the [speech] balloons and do the layouts. Then Kirby would tighten them up, and then most of the inking was mine. Not all, but a lot of it."

Simon and Kirby created Captain America for Timely Comics in the spring of 1941. His red, white, and blue costume, complete with star and stripes, mirrored the flag of the United States. The superhero's origins were patriotic as well. He was born Steve Rogers, a sickly boy. As a young man, Rogers was unable to pass his army physical exam. But his strong desire to serve his country draws the attention of the head of a secret army experiment. Rogers is given a special serum and bombarded with "vita-rays." The combination gives him extraordinary strength, coordination, and reflexes. Unfortunately, a Nazi spy kills the doctor in charge of the program before the doctor commits his research

Superman, Robin, and Batman joined forces to help the war effort during the early 1940s. Like many movie stars and sports figures, the comic book heroes urged Americans to buy U.S. government war bonds and stamps, which helped raise money for the U.S. military.

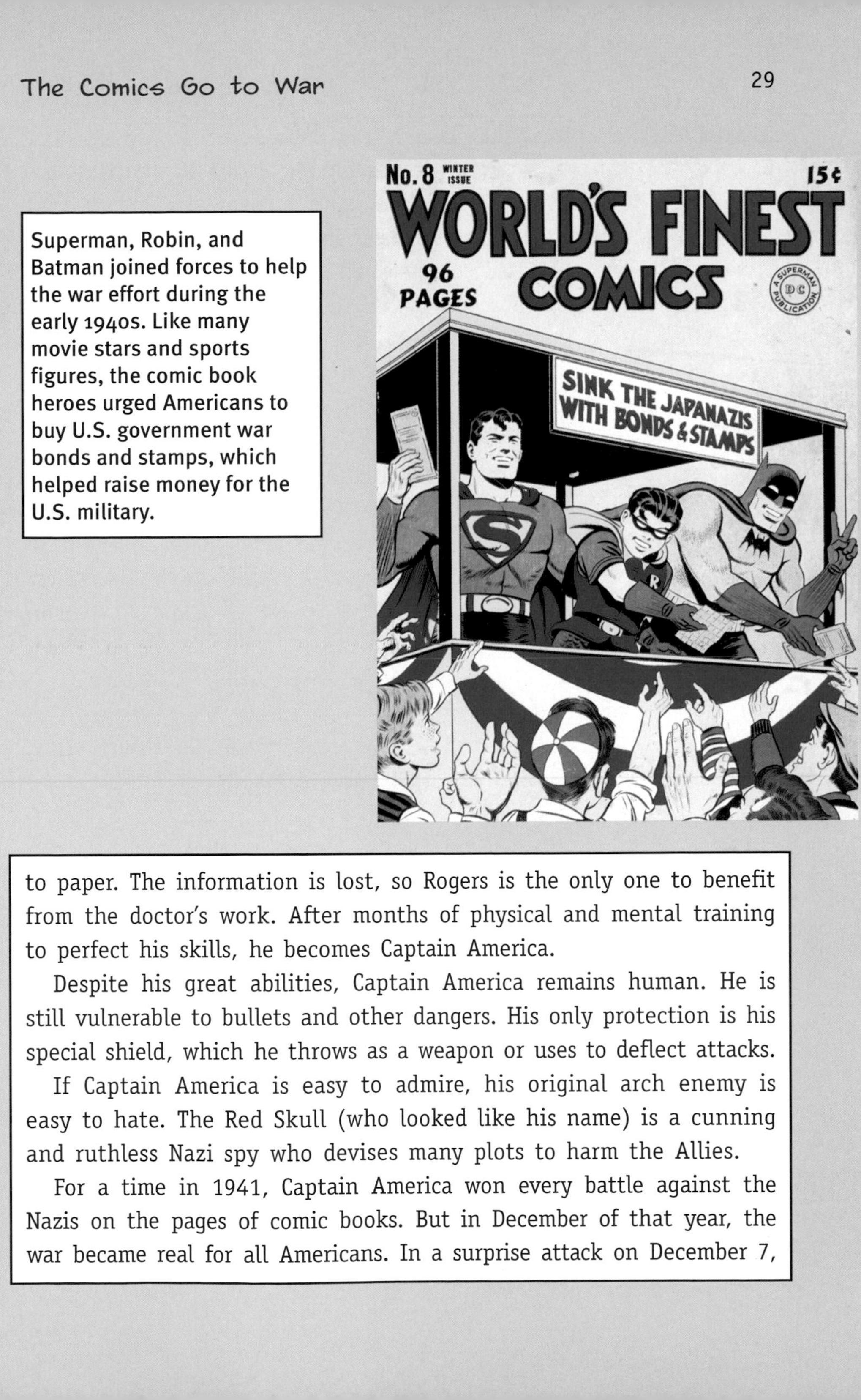
No. 8 WINTER ISSUE
15¢
WORLD'S FINEST COMICS
96 PAGES
A SUPERMAN PUBLICATION DC
SINK THE JAPANAZIS WITH BONDS & STAMPS

to paper. The information is lost, so Rogers is the only one to benefit from the doctor's work. After months of physical and mental training to perfect his skills, he becomes Captain America.

Despite his great abilities, Captain America remains human. He is still vulnerable to bullets and other dangers. His only protection is his special shield, which he throws as a weapon or uses to deflect attacks.

If Captain America is easy to admire, his original arch enemy is easy to hate. The Red Skull (who looked like his name) is a cunning and ruthless Nazi spy who devises many plots to harm the Allies.

For a time in 1941, Captain America won every battle against the Nazis on the pages of comic books. But in December of that year, the war became real for all Americans. In a surprise attack on December 7,

Japanese warplanes bombed U.S. military ships docked at the Pearl Harbor naval base in Hawaii. The next day, the United States declared war on Japan. In defense of Japan, Germany and Italy then declared war on the United States. Hundreds of thousands of U.S. soldiers began shipping out to fight in Europe and in the Pacific theater (battle region).

A Woman Takes Charge

As American men headed off to the battlefield, women's lives at home were transformed. Many went to work in wartime mills and factories, replacing the men fighting in uniform. Rosie the Riveter, a fictional female worker at a military factory, became a popular cartoon and

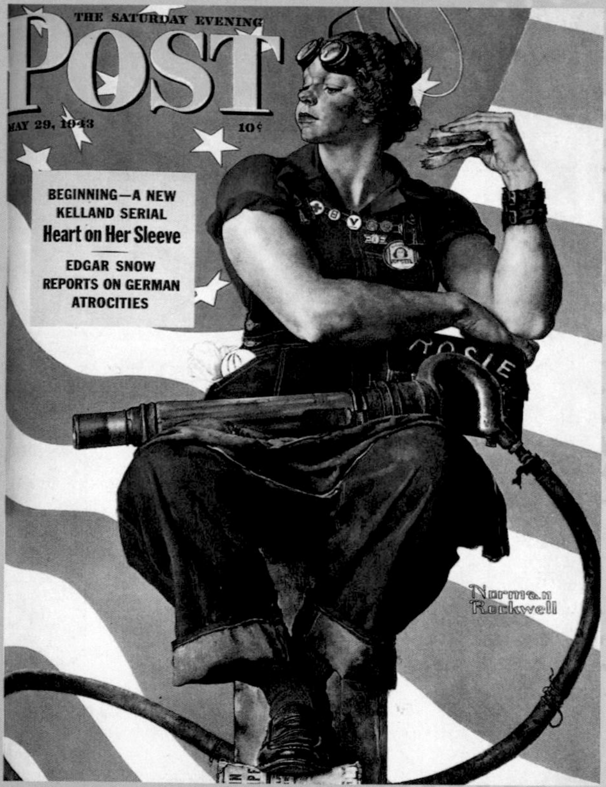
THE SATURDAY EVENING
POST
MAY 29, 1943
10¢
BEGINNING—A NEW KELLAND SERIAL
Heart on Her Sleeve
EDGAR SNOW REPORTS ON GERMAN ATROCITIES
ROSIE
Norman Rockwell

As American men enlisted in the armed forces, American women joined the work force in great numbers. Six million women took jobs in wartime factories making ammunition and building ships and airplanes. A common job was riveting—using drills and large bolts to piece together metal sheets. Using a song title for inspiration, illustrator Norman Rockwell paid tribute to all women workers by creating *Rosie the Riveter (left)* for a wartime cover of the *Saturday Evening Post* magazine.

poster image. Other women ran family farms and businesses and took up sole responsibility for their families' care. Under the circumstances, women made natural superheroes in the comic book world.

The first female superhero came from an unlikely source. William Moulton Marston was a Harvard-educated psychologist. In the early 1900s, Marston had done pioneering work studying the changes in people's blood pressure when they tell lies (which led to the invention of the first lie detectors). By middle age, Marston had become interested in the educational uses of comic books, and DC hired him as an adviser. At DC, Marston campaigned for a woman superhero, and in 1941, his boss at DC, Max Gaines, told him to go ahead and create his "wonder woman." Under the pen name Charles Moulton, Marston wrote his first Wonder Woman feature, which DC published in its *All-American All Star Comics* #8 that same year.

Marston's Wonder Woman was legendary. She wore America's star-spangled red, white, and blue. But her origins lay in Greek mythology. Her real name was Diana, and she came from a race of warrior women known as the Amazons. Her Amazon mother, Queen Hippolyta, had sculpted her from clay, and the Greek gods had brought her to life.

In Marston's story, the Amazons are ordered to find the greatest warrior among them to fight the schemes of the Greek war god, Ares. Queen Hippolyta forbids Diana from entering the competition that will identify the warrior. But Diana does so anyway—in disguise. When she wins, the queen allows her to undertake the mission, and Diana becomes Wonder Woman.

Along with her great strength and ability to fly, Wonder Woman can communicate telepathically with animals. Her costume includes bulletproof bracelets (good for warding off attacks) and a magic lasso. Anyone caught in the lasso has to answer questions truthfully.

After Wonder Woman defeats Ares, she goes on to fight other evil-doers. Marston continued to write the stories. And by the summer of 1942, Wonder Woman had become so popular with readers that DC created a separate Wonder Woman comic book.

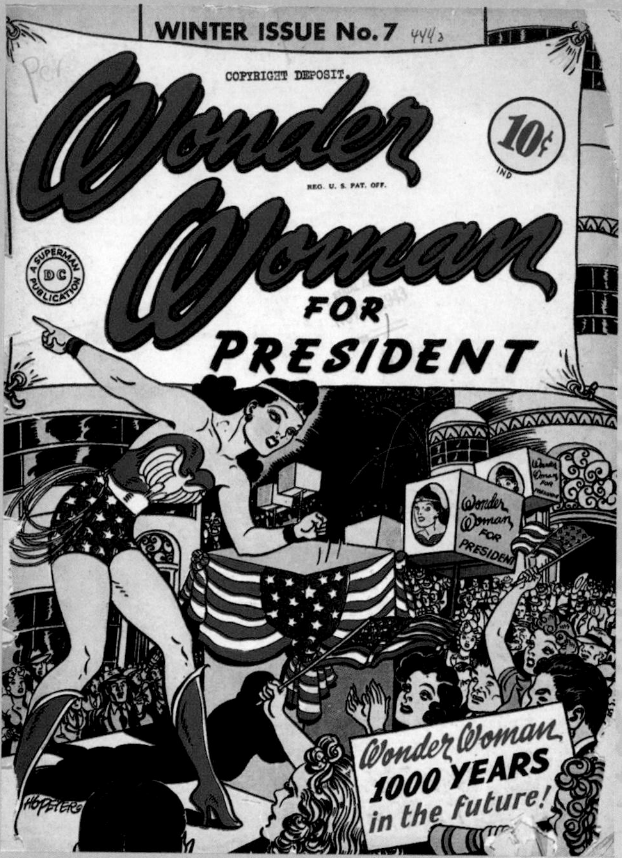
WINTER ISSUE No. 7
COPYRIGHT DEPOSIT.
Wonder Woman
10¢
REG. U. S. PAT. OFF.
A SUPERMAN DC PUBLICATION
FOR PRESIDENT
Wonder Woman FOR PRESIDENT
Wonder Woman 1000 YEARS in the future!

In a 1943 issue of *Wonder Woman*, William Marston imagined his heroine as a candidate for president of the United States. However, he imagined it at a safe distance—one thousand years in the future.

The Enlistment Grows

As the war continued, superheroes such as the Shield, Uncle Sam, and Captain Battle enlisted in the war effort. Clark Kent failed his eye exam and could not join the military, but Superman pitched in. In the comic book tales, most superheroes were not officially part of the military, but the military welcomed their assistance. And some had considerable resources of their own. Blackhawk, for example, is a Polish pilot who has somehow gained possession of a mysterious island. From there, he and his band of renegade pilots swoop in on the Nazis, upsetting their plans with aerial attacks.

In every instance, the purpose of these wartime stories was twofold. They were designed to entertain the reader, but they were also unabashedly patriotic. Everyone understood that fictional characters, whether superpowered or not, could not actually win the war. But as Matthew J. Pustz points out in *Comic Book Culture*, "Comics represented one way in which young readers could feel involved in the war effort. . . . Readers could . . . imagine themselves as their heroes, fighting the Nazis and the Japanese in the same way that their neighbors, older brothers, uncles, and fathers might have been doing. . . ."

Comic books were also taken overseas, where they helped raise the morale of the troops. The books were entertaining, portable, and easily replaced. Soldiers read and swapped them as they rested in camp or rode long hours in transport vehicles. The comic books reminded the soldiers of the things they used to do on lazy Sunday afternoons back home. Meanwhile, for the American public at home, the war-related comics gave them a fantasized glimpse of the war effort. On both fronts, the comics were doing their part to make victory seem possible.

A U.S. sailor aboard the USS *Doran* warship reads a comic book in a cabin lined with the ship's ammunition. Many World War II soldiers and sailors used comics to pass their off-duty time.

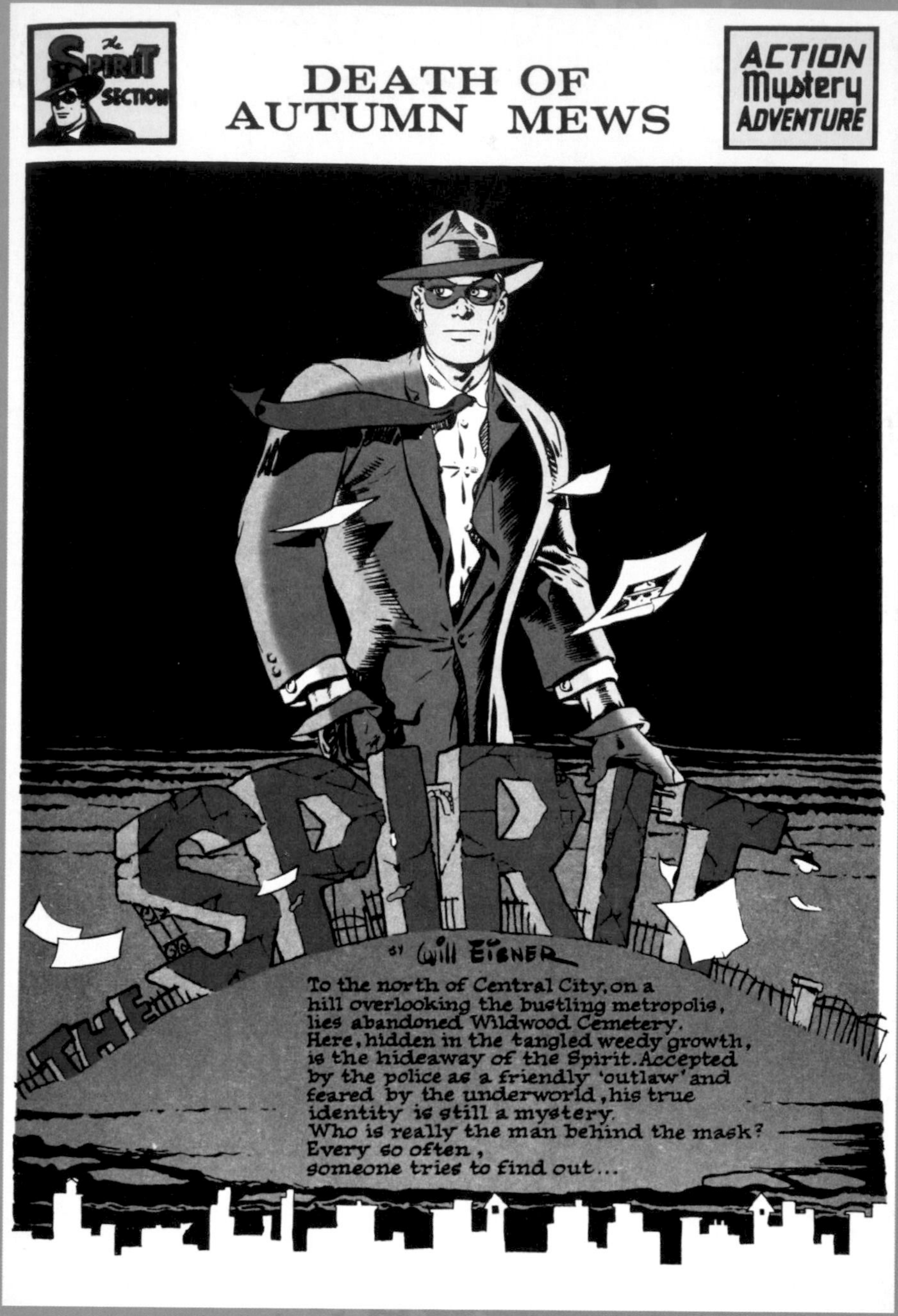
The Spirit Section
DEATH OF AUTUMN MEWS
ACTION Mystery ADVENTURE
THE SPIRIT
by Will Eisner
To the north of Central City, on a hill overlooking the bustling metropolis, lies abandoned Wildwood Cemetery. Here, hidden in the tangled weedy growth, is the hideaway of the Spirit. Accepted by the police as a friendly 'outlaw' and feared by the underworld, his true identity is still a mystery. Who is really the man behind the mask? Every so often, someone tries to find out...

Will Eisner's *The Spirit* began as a Sunday newspaper insert. Eisner felt that the series gave him a chance to show adult readers that comic books could feature complex characters and exciting storytelling.

THRIVING ON THE HOME FRONT

You may be dead, but by gosh, you're still a good cop!

—Police Commissioner Dolan to the Spirit, Comic Book Section, *June 1940*

As much as the war dominated American everyday life in the early 1940s, some things on the home front went on as usual. For example, some of the lighter genres popular at the very beginning of the comic book industry continued to find an audience. Old West stories set in the frontier communities of nineteenth-century America offered an alternative to futuristic superheroes. The rough-and-tumble of frontier towns, filled with gunslingers, dance hall girls, and Native Americans (usually portrayed as either loyal sidekicks or savage warriors), provided comic book writers and readers with a variety of plots and characters. Romance comic books—stories about the trials and drama of being in love—also had a sizable audience in the 1940s.

Adult and young readers loved comic books with cute talking animals, too, and during the war, the animals went right on being cute and talky. The most famous and enduring were cartoon characters—Mickey Mouse, Donald Duck, Woody Woodpecker, and Tom & Jerry—that had crossed over into comic books from the movies. Other successful characters of the era included Egbert the Elephant and Chester Chipmunk.

RAPID-FIRE, SMASH COLOR AND ACTION
10¢
WESTERN PICTURE STORIES
APRIL
WHITE MAN LEAVE TRAIL HERE!
BRILLIANT STORIES IN COLOR
RIDER of the PLAINS
COMPLETE IN THIS ISSUE
DRAGON PASS
by ARTHUR A. PINAJIAN
Also Stories By
DOWLING
BURLEY
EISNER

Western-themed comic books provided versatile story lines for 1940s readers. Characters included cowboys, Native Americans, gamblers, schoolmarms, and outlaws living on the U.S. western frontier of the nineteenth century.

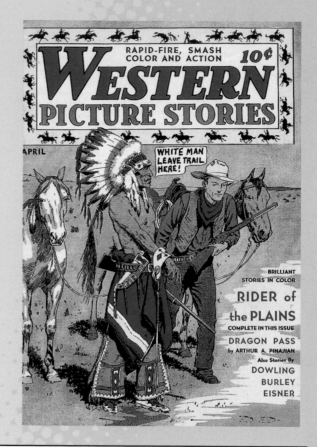

The All-American Teen

Along with all these cowboys, lovers, and funny animals, was there room for even more light reading material? John Goldwater, a partner in MLJ Magazines, thought so. Goldwater's idea was simple. Instead of trying to create characters that readers could fantasize about, why not create characters who were more like the readers themselves?

Goldwater modeled his new idea on the popular Andy Hardy movies that starred the young actor Mickey Rooney. Fourteen Andy Hardy movies were made during the late 1930s and the 1940s, including *Life Begins for Andy Hardy* and *Love Laughs at Andy Hardy*. Andy was supposed to be a typical American teenager. He got into

Andy Hardy (Mickey Rooney) finds himself in another mix-up with a girl (June Preisser) in *Judge Hardy and Son* (1939).

mischief and forgot to do his homework. Girls were the biggest problem—and delight—for Andy. (In fact, in *Andy Hardy's Double Life*, Andy thinks he's gotten himself engaged to two girls at once.)

Since moviegoers were also comic book readers, Goldwater figured he had a built-in audience. He began planning Archie Comics, a comic book series that followed the adventures of a group of teenagers in the fictional all-American town of Riverdale. The series was written by Vic Bloom and drawn by Bob Montana. It first appeared in an issue of *Pep Comics* in 1941. The title character, Archie Andrews, spends most of his time goofing around with his friend Jughead and trying to outwit his rival, Reggie. Archie is pursued by Betty Cooper, the pretty girl next door. Unfortunately for Betty, Archie has a crush on Veronica Lodge, the daughter of the local millionaire.

The antics and escapades of Archie and his friends were about as controversial as milk and cookies, but that was OK. In fact, it was more than OK. With all the craziness going on in the world, it was refreshing to visit a place where the biggest worry was finding a date for Saturday night.

NO. 1
The Mirth of a Nation
MLJ
Archie
comics
10¢
ISN'T ARCHIE A WONDERFUL SKATER?
YES! BUT CAN HE SWIM!
ALSO
CUBBY THE BEAR
JUDGE OWL
SQUOIMY THE WOIM
BUMBIE THE BEE-TECTIVE

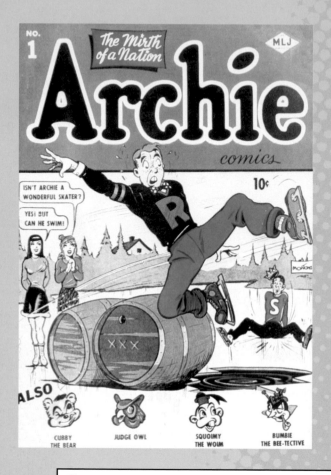

The Andy Hardy movies inspired comic book publisher John Goldwater to develop his own humorous teenage hero. Like Andy Hardy, Archie Andrews *(left)* is an average high-school kid who gets crushes on girls, worries his parents, and annoys his teachers.

Swamp Creatures

As Archie and his pals carried out their teenage exploits in Riverdale, another comic book series, *Pogo*, took an amusing but more thoughtful look at American life. The title character of *Pogo* was a kind and happy-go-lucky possum. The creation of Walt Kelly, Pogo first appeared in *Animal Comics* in 1943. The possum lived in Georgia's Okefenokee Swamp with his friends, including Albert Alligator, Howland Owl, and the turtle Churchy LaFemme. The goings-on in the swamp were then also published in newspaper comic strips.

The southern U.S. accents and the comic antics of the animals made

*EVVYBUDDY DONE WORKED ON OUAH NEW BOAT BUT **YOU**—YOU IS A LOAFER!*

*WHUT IN DE WORL' IS DE MATTAH WIF DAT? EVVY PLACE IN DE KENTRY GOT HER **BUMS** AND **NO-GOODS!** AH IS MERE KEEPIN UP APPEARANCES— AH IS DE **BUM** OF DE SWAMP.*

Pogo Possum *(left)* **first appeared as a character in a 1943 comic book. But as Pogo's creator, Walt Kelly, got into the newspaper business, he began writing *Pogo* as a daily comic strip. The strip proved so successful that Kelly's good-natured possum was soon back in comic books, this time in a starring role.**

Pogo popular. But Kelly's animals were not just cute and funny. They were all unique and detailed characters, and Kelly often used them to analyze or poke fun at social issues, such as politics and education.

MEAN STREETS AND HARD HEARTS

Representing the darker side of home front life was the crime genre. Crime was a popular comic book subject even when it did not involve any superheroes. Realistic crime stories had been part of comic books from the beginning. Naturally, the crimes were never peacefully executed. There were gun battles and car chases. There were damsels in distress and gangsters' molls, all of whom looked good even when they were very bad. Many of these comics were packaged as a series. The key word in their titles was *crime*. Such titles included *True Crime, March of Crime, Crime SuspenStories,* and *Crime Exposed*. Most popular of all was *Crime Does Not Pay*, which ironically did pay very well for its publishing company, Comic House, and the publisher Lev Gleason.

Prominent among the creators of this crime genre were Charles Biro and Bob Wood. Both were already comic book artists when Gleason first paired them up to create *Crime Does Not Pay*. The series featured non-fiction stories about the worst criminals of the day and fiction plots containing the most evil ideas the writers could invent. In superhero comic books, readers always sensed that the villains and their dastardly schemes were all make-believe. But the crime story comics were mean and nasty. They were meant to entertain by shocking readers.

A Spiritual Awakening

The characters in crime stories often were not psychologically deep or realistic. The crime itself—murder, robbery, blackmail—was the star of the story. But while that trend continued in general, a more complex crime figure also appeared. He was known as the Spirit. His creator was Will Eisner, a comics writer and artist. Eisner had worked with many comic book pioneers, including Jack Kirby and Bob Kane. He had even turned down an offer to work on an early version of Superman.

The Spirit first appeared in June 1940, in a syndicated newspaper supplement called the *Weekly Comic Book*. The supplement, inserted into Sunday papers, was a way for newspapers to share in the success of comic books. The Des Moines Register and Tribune Syndicate approached Eisner about creating a character for the *Weekly Comic Book*, and Eisner saw the offer as a chance to create a more sophisticated hero for older readers.

The Spirit is a masked detective who lives in the imaginary Central City (often thought to be modeled after New York City, where Eisner grew up). Most of the other characters in the stories do not know who the Spirit is or where he comes from. "[He] is really Denny Colt," explained Eisner, "a young criminologist presumed dead by the public but who continues to assist society behind the mask of the Spirit. That he operates out of Wildwood Cemetery, where he is supposed to be buried, is known only to [Police] Commissioner Dolan and his daughter Ellen. . . ."

Will Eisner's *The Spirit* was often moody and atmospheric—fitting well with the theme of a lonely hero whom everyone thinks is dead.

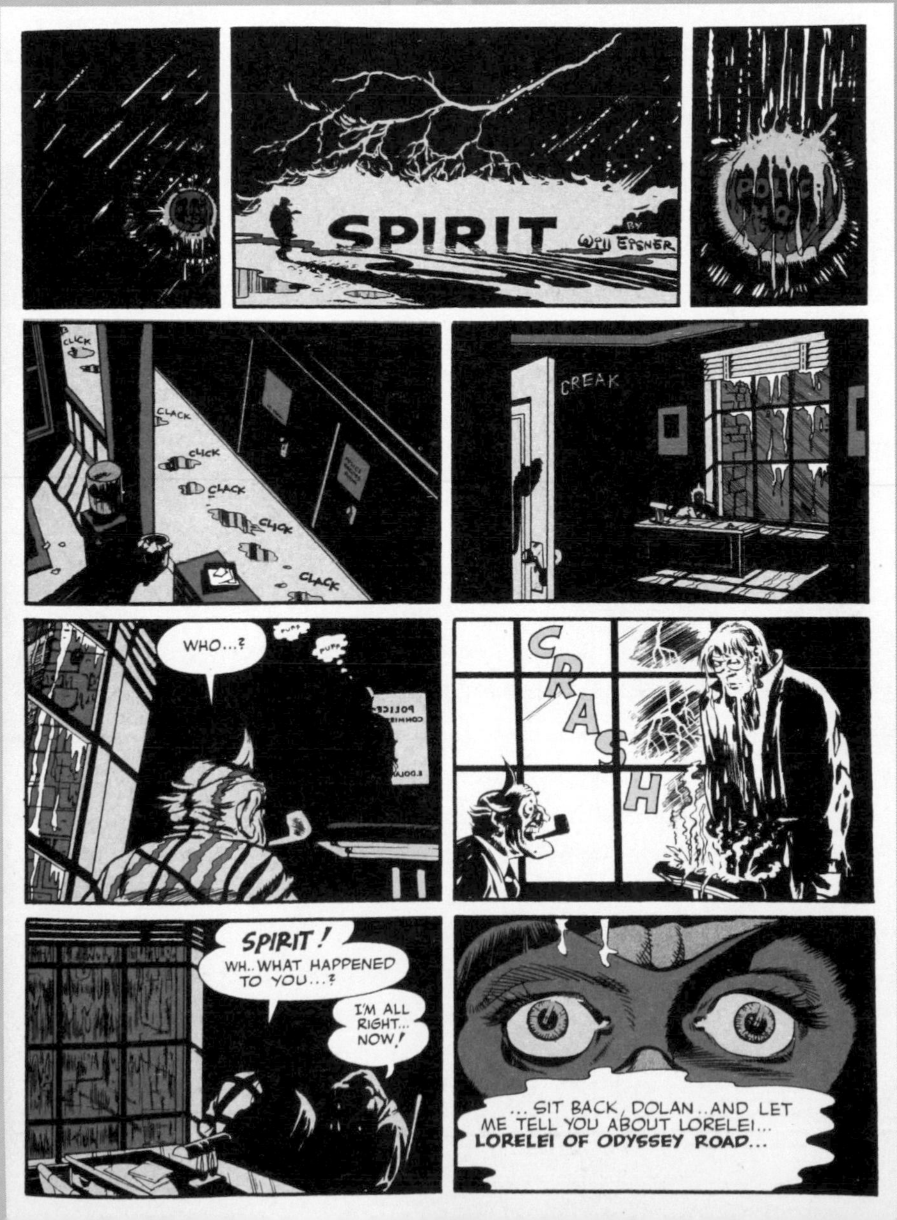
SPIRIT
BY WILL EISNER
CLICK
CLACK
CLICK
CLACK
CLICK
CLACK
CREAK
WHO...?
PUFF
PUFF
CRASH
SPIRIT! WH..WHAT HAPPENED TO YOU...?
I'M ALL RIGHT... NOW!
... SIT BACK, DOLAN..AND LET ME TELL YOU ABOUT LORELEI... LORELEI OF ODYSSEY ROAD...

Eisner did not want his character to be a run-of-the-mill super-hero. The Spirit has no superpowers or amazing gadgets. He does not wear a costume and has no capes or fancy symbols on his clothes. Eisner dressed the Spirit in a dark blue business suit and a wide-brimmed hat. The Spirit wore a blue eye mask only to conceal his identity. He uses his smarts and his toughness to help fight crime on the streets of Central City.

The Spirit is an unusual character, more like a detective than a superhero. But what made the strip really distinctive was Eisner's approach to storytelling. His illustrated panels often looked like scenes from a movie. Many comic book scenes at the time were drawn from a straight-on point of view, with bright colors and simple actions. But panels from *The Spirit* were drawn from unusual angles and with dramatic lighting. In one scene, a half-open door sheds a long triangle of harsh light on a shabby police office. In another, the Spirit trudges down a broken sidewalk past shadowy doorways swept with rain. In making these creative choices, Eisner was influenced by film noir, a style of moviemaking common in crime and mystery dramas of the era. And as in these movies, Eisner often used a character's vivid facial expressions to tell readers more than dialogue ever could.

The Spirit was Eisner's creation, but he did not work alone. Help-ing him produce the *Weekly Comic Book* stories was a team of tal-ented artists. The team included artist Jules Feiffer, who went on to achieve his own fame as a cartoonist, playwright, and movie screen-writer. In his book, *The Great Comic Book Heroes*, Feiffer summed up the way hero and superhero faces such as the Spirit's were drawn: "sharp, slanting eyebrows, thick at the ends, thinning out toward the nose, of which in three-quarter view there was hardly any—just a small V placed slightly above the mouth, casting the faintest nick of a shadow. One never saw a nose full view. . . . [Noses] were too hard to draw. Eyes were usually ball-less, two thin slits. Mouths were always thick, quick single lines—never double. Mouths, for some

Jules Feiffer was one of the primary artists on *The Spirit*.

reason, were rarely shown open. Dialogue, theoretically, was spoken from the nose. Heroes' faces were square-jawed; in some cases, all jawed. Often there was a cleft in the chin."

The Spirit's look and content proved successful, and soon five million readers were following the character's adventures each week. In 1942 *The Spirit* became a traditional comic book as well. Even while Eisner served in the army during World War II, his production team kept the stories coming. The long-running series set a new standard in comic book art. "As a comic book artist I continually look to Will Eisner's work for inspiration—in particular his groundbreaking work in *The Spirit*," says Bill Hauser of Minneapolis, Minnesota. "His imaginative layouts and dynamic sense of storytelling have seldom been equaled in the medium of comics."

The darkened mean streets of *The Spirit* and the sunny suburban lawns of *Archie Comics* were about as far apart on looks and themes as they could be. But both comics' character types—the imperfect hero who does things his own way and the fun-loving teenager—carried over successfully to the next era in comic books.

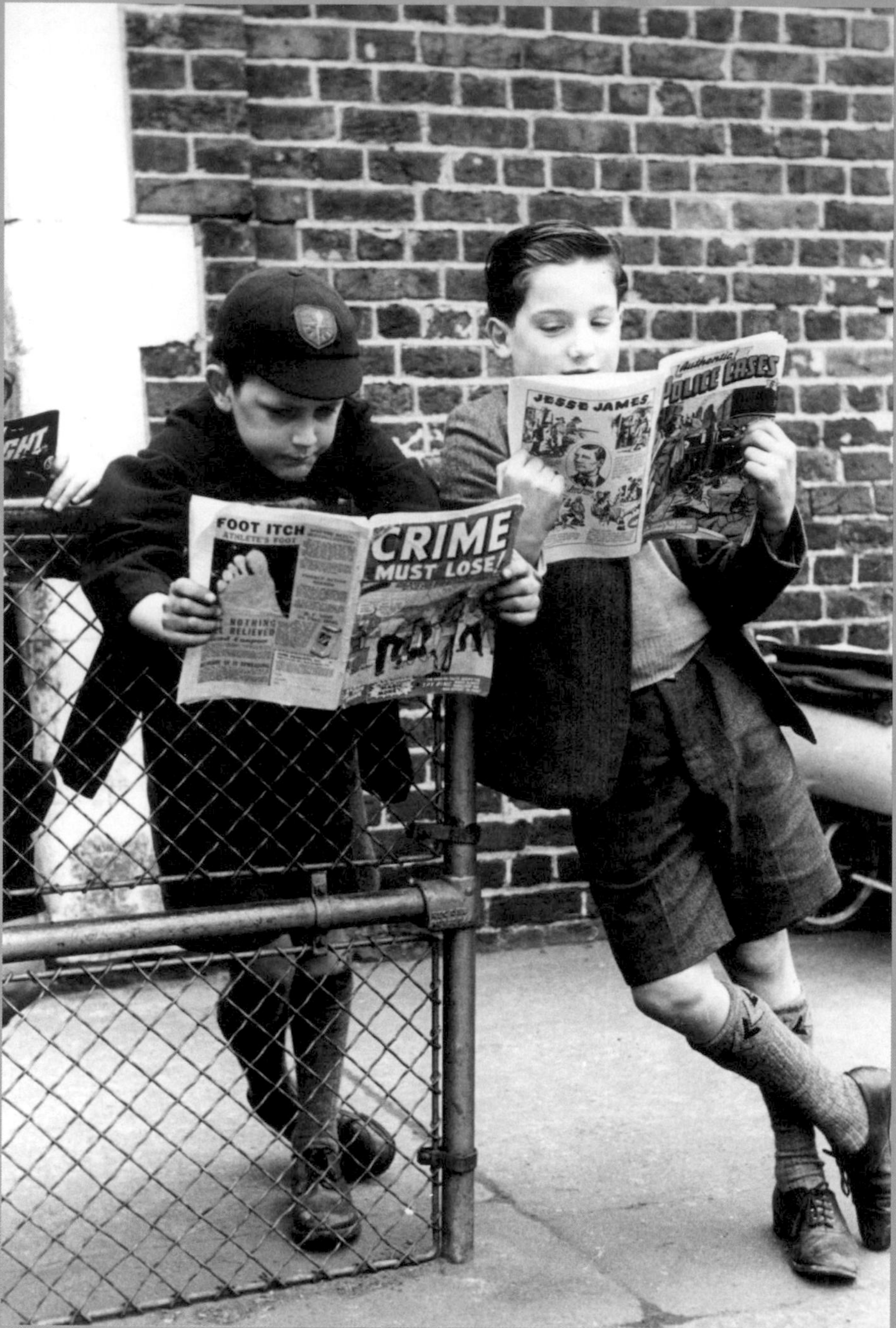
FOOT ITCH
ATHLETE'S FOOT
CRIME
MUST LOSE!
JESSE JAMES
Authentic
POLICE CASES

Two American children in the early 1950s are shown reading crime comic books. In the post-World War II era, U.S. officials worried (as they had in the past) about the causes of juvenile delinquency. Comic books depicting violent crime and sexual themes were cited as a bad influence on young minds.

Comics Under Fire

All lurid, unsavory, gruesome illustrations shall be eliminated.

—*Comics Code Authority of 1954*

World War II ended in 1945 with an Allied victory, and soldiers began coming home. Many soldiers had joined the service as teens and upon returning home, they attended college. Others, already married or planning on marrying soon, purchased new homes. The war had boosted the U.S. economy, and many workers found it easy to find good jobs. With money in the bank and new homes in rapidly growing suburbs, many young American couples felt ready to begin large families. They had a sense of well-being and optimism about the future, which triggered what has come to be called the baby boom—a huge increase in the number of children born in the United States in the years following the war.

In the 1950s, the first of the baby boom children grew into adolescents. Unlike their parents' generation, many of the baby boomers did not have to worry about economic hardship. They were carefree and often had plenty of spending money. They created a youth culture with its own clothes and lingo. They danced to a new sound—too loud and wild for their parents—called rock 'n' roll music. They watched movies made just for them, featuring teenage characters—serious movies such as *Rebel without a Cause* or lighthearted films such

Two American teenagers enjoy milkshakes at their local hangout in 1954. Many teenagers benefited from post-war U.S. prosperity. With little need to contribute to family chores or finances, the teens had plenty of leisure time and spending money.

as Elvis Presley's *King Creole*. Looking back at the 1950s, the youth culture resembles a sock-hopping, pizza-eating, jalopy-driving picture of white, middle-class prosperity—an issue of Archie Comics come to life.

But many other things were happening in the United States in the 1950s. African Americans were fighting against discrimination in education, housing, and employment. Women, too, were seeking equality in education and on the job. And many European immigrants, displaced by World War II, were struggling to begin new lives in the United States.

THE COLD WAR

Farther from home, there were big problems too. World War II was over, but global political tensions remained. The Soviet Union (USSR) had been part of the Allied force that defeated Nazi Germany. But after the war, the USSR faced an enormous political divide with its former allies. Unlike the Western free-market democracies of Great Britain, France, and the United States, the USSR was a Communist country. The Soviet government controlled all aspects of its economy. The USSR had installed Communist leaders in several East Europe countries, and it wanted to convert more countries to Communism. The Allies, especially the United States, wanted to stop the Soviet expansionist push. The tensions between the USSR and Western democracies became known as the Cold War.

The Cold War never broke out into actual battles between the United States and the USSR. But it spurred an intense and frightening arms race between the two countries. Both superpowers rushed to build bigger and better weapons. The United States had used powerful atomic bombs against Japan at the end of World War II, and as the Cold War intensified, people grew afraid that nuclear weapons would be used again.

Many Americans also feared that Soviet spies or agents were working within the United States to take over the country. Senator Joseph McCarthy of Wisconsin claimed that dangerous Communists were working within the U.S. government and military. McCarthy led U.S. Senate hearings in 1953 and 1954 to investigate the Communist threat. The Senate hearings and similar hearings forced people—military workers, teachers, scientists, writers, entertainers, and others—to defend their political beliefs against charges of disloyalty to the United States. Being a member of the Communist Party was not (and still is not) against the law, but Cold War fears were so strong that many people shared McCarthy's fierce anti-Communist feelings. In this climate, many Americans were persecuted for their political views, not for any crimes they actually committed.

THE SEDUCTION OF THE INNOCENT

Not all Americans were checking under their beds for Communist spies. Yet many people were concerned about other serious problems. Violent street crime and juvenile delinquency (crimes such as vandalism and fighting committed by young people), for example, were on the rise in the United States. Americans began to question the root causes of these issues.

Well-known psychiatrist Dr. Frederic Wertham criticized the negative effect of popular culture on young people. Wertham believed that violence in movies, on radio programs, and in popular reading material contributed to youthful crime and to antisocial attitudes in general. Wertham turned particular attention to comic books. Crime, horror, and superhero comics were filled with violent fights, scantily clad women, and even brutal murders shown in detail. Wertham also argued that African Americans and other minorities were often depicted in comics as "inferior and subhuman." Moreover, kids could buy and read comic books on their own—digesting these violent and racist images without the permission or guidance of parents, teachers, or librarians.

Many people, including influential politicians, agreed with Wertham. Some communities began protesting against and even banning certain comic books. Alarmed by this trend, comic book companies formed their own editorial boards to curb depictions of violence and sexual aggression or promiscuity. Several industry leaders came together to create the Association of Comic Magazine Publishers (ACMP) to set some standards and to improve the comic book image.

But ACMP's efforts to regulate the entire industry were less than a complete success. Large publishers such as DC and Dell did not join ACMP. They chose to rely on their own editorial boards. And other publishers simply did not agree with the code. Some argued that the horror and crime comics were meant for adults—it was up to parents, not publishers, to keep inappropriate material out of kids' hands. Other comic book publishers simply followed the trail of financial success. If "bad" comics were selling, they would keep publishing them.

Public pressure, however, continued to mount. In 1954 Wertham published a full-length book, *The Seduction of the Innocent*. He made his view plain. "All comic books with their words and expletives

In Norwich, Connecticut, two children add to a pile of comic books in the back of a pickup truck. The comic books are destined to be burned in a bonfire held by a local women's group. In the mid-1950s, community groups organized bonfires and other protests to express their anger about the violent and sexual content of some comic books.

[swear words] in balloons are bad for reading," he wrote in the first chapter, "but not every comic book is bad for children's minds and emotions. The trouble is that the 'good' comic books are snowed under by those which glorify violence [and] crime."

In Wertham's view, many comic books were not simply a harmless waste of time. They encouraged people, especially children, to take part in destructive acts and violent crimes. Other experts disagreed. They thought comic books could not drive normal, well-adjusted kids to commit violent crimes. More likely, violent images and stories were harmful influences on children who were already troubled. But to whatever extent they agreed with Wertham, many parents, educators, and religious leaders pushed for changes in comic book regulation.

When the uproar grew loud enough, politicians started paying attention. The U.S. Senate held investigative committee hearings in 1954 and invited several leading publishers to defend their comic books. EC Comics publisher William Gaines (son of Max Gaines) gained newspaper notoriety for his remarks before the committee. When called to testify, Gaines insisted that he only published comic books that were "in good taste." At that point, Senator Estes Kefauver of Tennessee held up an issue of an EC Comics, and asked, "This seems to be a man with a bloody axe holding a woman's head up, which has been severed from her body. Do you think that's in good taste?" Gaines answered, "Yes, sir, I do—for the cover of a horror comic." The exchange made front-page news in the *New York Times* the next morning.

HORROR
THE VAULT OF HORROR
NO. 37
JULY
10¢
FEATURING...
THE VAULT-KEEPER
THE CRYPT-KEEPER
THE OLD WITCH

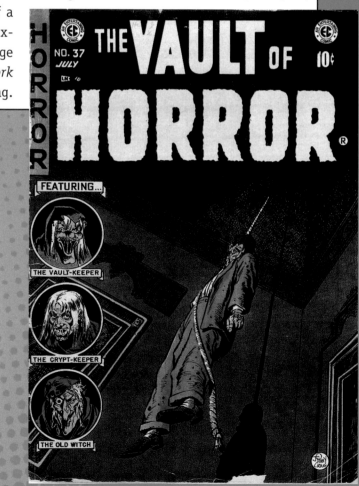

***The Vault of Horror* *(right)* is an EC comic book from the early 1950s. EC Comics published crime and horror comics. Many of them were violent and bloody, featuring people being beaten or even killed. This brought EC to the attention of a U.S. Senate committee on juvenile delinquency.**

Under the U.S. constitutional right of freedom of speech, comic book companies knew they could keep publishing whatever they wanted. But what was the point if no one would buy what they printed? They were, after all, in business to make money. Realizing they had lost the public's support and trust, the publishers searched for a way to get it back. In late 1954, comic book publishers formed a new organization, the Comics Magazine Association of America (CMAA). More important, they created the Comics Code Authority (CCA), a seal of approval whose logo would appear on the cover of approved comics from then on.

To get this approval, a comic book had to follow a long list of CMAA guidelines. These guidelines limited the tone and direction that stories could follow. Among its provisions were the following:

- Crimes shall never be presented in such a way as to create sympathy for the criminal.
- Policemen, judges, government officials, and respected institutions shall never be presented in such a way as to create disrespect for established authority.
- In every instance good shall triumph over evil and the criminal punished for his misdeeds.
- All lurid, unsavory, gruesome illustrations shall be eliminated.

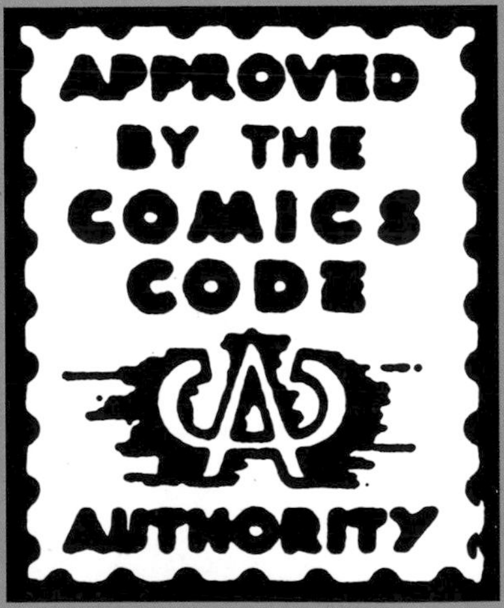
APPROVED
BY THE
COMICS
CODE
CA
AUTHORITY

Starting in 1954, comic book publishers submitted their comics to the CCA to receive a seal of approval *(left)*. The seal was printed on the covers of approved books, assuring comic book sellers and parents that the books were suitable for young readers.

Not every publisher joined the CMAA, but they were all affected by it. One holdout, Gaines, discontinued his horror and crime comic books "because of a premise that has never been proved, that they stimulate juvenile delinquency. We are not doing so [discontinuing the books] as much for business reasons as because this seems to be what parents want—and parents should be served." However, Gaines also knew that these comic books would no longer sell.

CHANGING COURSES IN MIDSTREAM

The change in the industry brought a dramatic shift in sales. As Ron Goulart reported in *Great American Comic Books*, about five hundred different comic book titles had been published before the Wertham controversy and Senate hearings. By 1955 that number had fallen to about three hundred DC Comics had combined monthly sales of 10.5 million copies in 1955. Two years later, that number had fallen by more than one-half. The decline at Timely was even more dramatic— from 15 million copies in 1953 to 4.6 million in 1958.

Some publishers simply got out of the business completely. Others scrambled to find new subjects to take the place of crime and horror stories. Some new titles, for example, featured comics based on pleasant but bland movie stars such as Bob Hope and Roy Rogers. At DC, editor Julius Schwartz created a new version of the Flash. With the prohibitions on fighting and violence, Schwartz relied on new design elements focused on the Flash's dynamic costume and the way his super speed was presented visually across the page.

As more of the baby boom generation reached reading age, more attention was paid to comics for younger readers. Animated movie cartoons continued to spin off into comic books. Harvey Comics published gentle characters such as Casper the Friendly Ghost and Richie Rich. Series such as *Classics Illustrated* recreated famous works of literature as comic books for young readers. And successful newspaper comic strips such as *Dennis the Menace* branched out into books.

Science fiction also survived—or even thrived—in a less violent form. The launch of the Soviet satellite *Sputnik* in 1957 and the space race with the United States made looking out into the galaxy feel very different. The early 1950s had seen violent story lines set on different planets or in the future. But the reach of the comics code extended over time and space. As a result, science fiction of the late 1950s focused more on character and personality and less on zapping with ray guns. Series such as *Mystery in Space* and *Space Adventure* offered a softer kind of intergalactic adventure story.

Still, there was no question that comic books had taken a hit—the kind that in their own pages would have been drawn with big, bold letters. Could they recover? The one certain thing was that they would not go down without a fight.

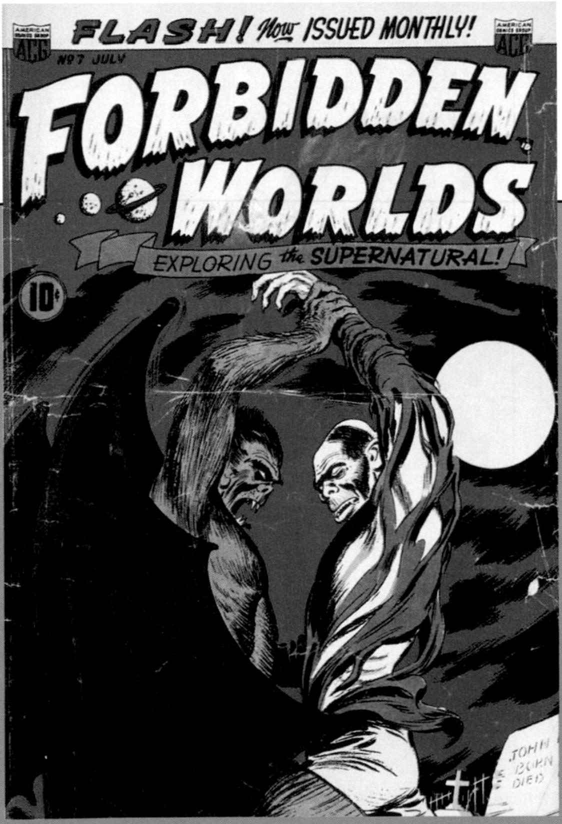
FLASH! Now ISSUED MONTHLY!
AMERICAN COMICS GROUP ACG
No 7 JULY
FORBIDDEN WORLDS
EXPLORING the SUPERNATURAL!
10¢

In the late 1950s, comic books such as *Forbidden Worlds* combined elements of science fiction and tales of the supernatural.

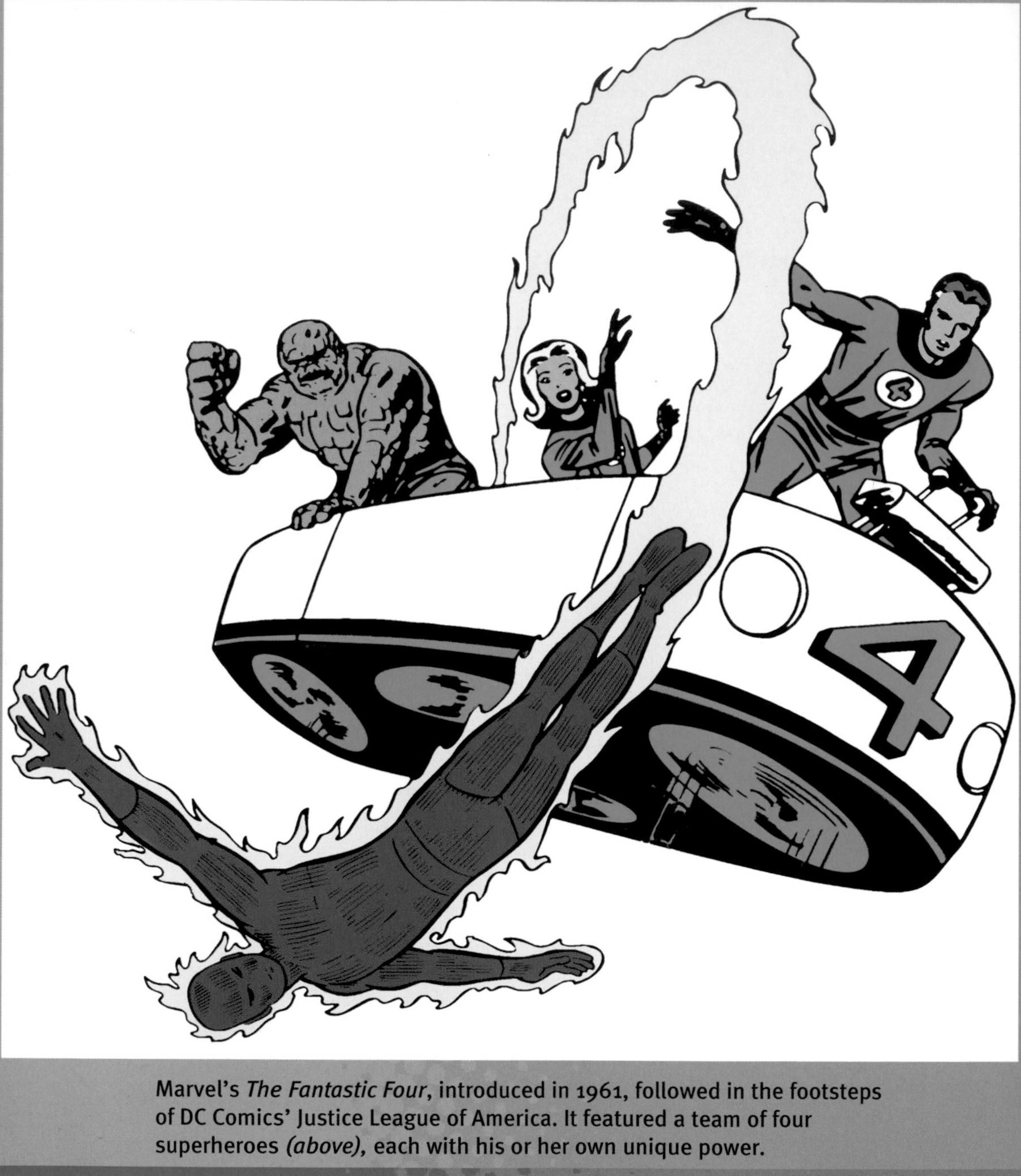

Marvel's *The Fantastic Four*, introduced in 1961, followed in the footsteps of DC Comics' Justice League of America. It featured a team of four superheroes *(above)*, each with his or her own unique power.

A NEW ERA

> *With the sudden fury of a thunderbolt, a flare is shot into the sky over Central City. Three awesome words take form as if by magic, and a legend is born!*
>
> —The Fantastic Four #1, November 1961

In 1960 John F. Kennedy, a senator from Massachusetts, was elected president of the United States. At forty-three, Kennedy was the youngest president ever elected and the first one to be born in the twentieth century. His election was hailed as the beginning of a new era, and he and his glamorous family were seen as a breath of fresh air in the White House. Kennedy and his wife, Jackie, were charming and sophisticated. The Kennedy children, Caroline and John Jr.—the first young children to be raised in the White House in fifty years—were famously photographed skipping across the carpet in the presidential Oval Office. But beyond his youthful image, Kennedy was a serious politician. He promoted fresh ideas ranging from the Peace Corps (a volunteer group that works with people in poor countries) to the bold promise of putting an American on the moon in less than ten years.

Kennedy's presidency looked optimistically and energetically to the future. In this, Kennedy encouraged but also reflected the mood of the country. The Cold War was still deadly serious business. But baby boomers entering adulthood wanted something more, as they saw it, than their parents' fears about Communists and their desires for perfect suburban homes. The most ambitious among them wanted to change the world for the better.

Stymied by the comics code, the world of comic books seemed to have trouble keeping up. The code sapped energy out of the potential for exciting, new story lines and drove many creative people away from the field. And television had arrived on the scene, grabbing the attention of the comic book audience. For many people, children in particular, watching an adventure or comedy on the small black-and-white screen was more appealing than reading about one in colored panels on the printed page.

A Fantastic Chain Reaction

Like many of his comic book colleagues, writer Stanley Lieber was discouraged about his prospects. He had first entered the comic book business as a teenager. He planned to stay only a few years. Without any real sense of direction, he ended up writing whatever he was told for his employer. He later recalled what it was like working for Martin Goodman, who ran the company named, at various times, Timely, Atlas, and Marvel Comics. "Whatever was selling at the moment—[Goodman] would publish books in that genre. For instance, when it looked as though Westerns were hot . . . we added a lot of Western titles. When Romance stories were doing well . . . we published a lot of Romance books. Then we did a lot of War magazines. Then Horror. Then Crime. Then the Animated-type of characters. . . . We did Teenage titles. We never were leaders in the field—we always followed the trends."

By the early sixties, Lieber was in his thirties. He had written a number of stories under the pen name Stan Lee, but none had ever made much of a splash. So when Martin Goodman asked him to come up with an idea for a group of superheroes, Lieber figured he had nothing to lose by trying something different. Goodman had asked Lieber for the idea because DC Comics—Marvel's rival—was having great success with its Justice League of America (in which Superman, Batman, Wonder Woman, and others shared adventures).

Lieber's wife, Joan, encouraged him to take the leap. "Joan wanted

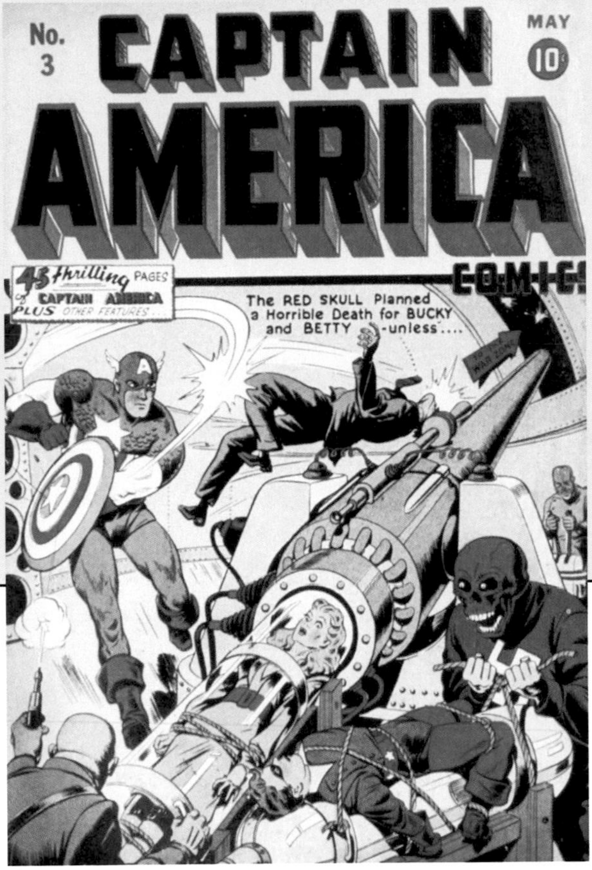
No. 3
CAPTAIN AMERICA
COMIC
MAY
10¢
43 thrilling PAGES of CAPTAIN AMERICA PLUS OTHER FEATURES
The RED SKULL Planned a Horrible Death for BUCKY and BETTY -unless....

Jack Kirby and Stan Lee worked together at Timely Comics (later Marvel Comics) on *Captain America* and other titles. By the early 1960s, both men were looking for fresh, new characters and stories.

me to bear down and make something of myself in the comic book field," Lieber said. "She wondered why I did not put as much effort and creativity into the comics as I seemed to be putting into my other freelance endeavors. The fact is, I had always thought of my comic book work as a temporary job—even after all those years—and her little dissertation made me suddenly realize that it was time to start concentrating on what I was doing—to carve a real career for myself in the nowhere world of comic books."

Adopting his pen name permanently, Lee decided to shake things up a little. It was clear to him that many of the traditional superhero starting points had become stale. He discussed his new ideas with Jack Kirby, an artist who worked with Marvel and other comics publishers. Kirby had created Captain America and many other characters, but he had fallen into a rut, feeling the future of comic books was bleak. Working with Lee on a new group of superheroes fired his imagination again.

Lee and Kirby's original story concerned four astronauts in an experimental rocket. They are unexpectedly bombarded with cosmic rays, which affect each of them differently. Their leader, Reed Richards, acquires the ability to stretch all parts of his body. His girlfriend, Sue Storm, finds that she can become invisible and project a force field. Sue's teenage brother, Johnny, becomes a human torch (like the Human Torch of the early 1940s). And pilot Ben Grimm becomes a rocklike creature with great strength and toughness. The four adopt superhero names: Mister Fantastic (Reed), the Invisible Woman (Sue), the Human Torch (Johnny), and the Thing (Ben).

In creating the Fantastic Four, Lee relied on some superhero conventions, such as superpowers and alter egos. But he added his own twists. Lee explained in a later interview that ordinary people in the stories know exactly who the Fantastic Four are, "instead of the typical heroes that have secret identities." Two of the four are related, two are in love, and all four are close friends. Each has flaws and personal problems, which only makes them more interesting. Lee also strived for natural, realistic dialogue, and Kirby drew the heroes looking as if they did not invest a lot of thought in colorful tights-and-capes outfits. Initially, in fact, the Fantastic Four wore regular clothes. "I always felt that if I had super-power," Lee explained, "I wouldn't immediately run out to the store and buy a costume."

The Fantastic Four's first issue appeared in November 1961. For Lee, the reaction came as a big surprise. Readers got a kick out of the Fantastic Four. They liked seeing Reed and Sue bicker, Johnny annoying everyone, and Ben being grumpy while the four of them battled evildoers such as Dr. Doom. Lee had been ready to leave the comics field, but the positive response to his new creation was so overwhelming that he stayed on. And Kirby's vivid illustrations created a whole new style for Marvel. Together, Lee's natural dialogue

THE WORLD'S GREATEST COMIC MAGAZINE!
12¢
THE Fantastic FOUR
4 MAY
STOP HIM! IF THE SUB-MARINER REACHES THE WATER, HE'LL BECOME INVINCIBLE!
"THE COMING OF THE SUB-MARINER!"

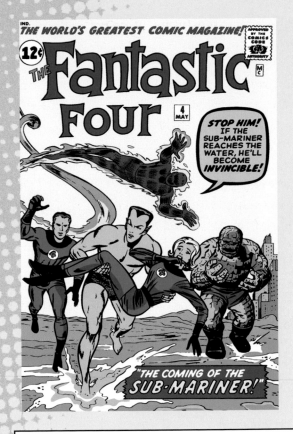

The Sub-Mariner joined *The Fantastic Four* for several issues beginning in 1962. The Sub-Mariner acted as an anti-hero, a character who is not a villain but who often does not act very heroic either. In the issue shown at left, the Sub-Mariner kidnaps Sue Storm.

and flawed characters appealed to 1960s kids looking to "get real," while Kirby's imaginative art matched the colorful, loose style of the times. This fresh approach to superhero comics kicked off what has come to be called the Silver Age of Comic Books.

Radiation and More Radiation

With the Fantastic Four, Lee was just getting started. In 1962, when harmful radiation from U.S. nuclear bomb testing was often in the news, he and Kirby introduced another unlikely superhero—the Incredible Hulk. If the Thing was a bit rough around the edges, the Hulk was as close to a monster as a superhero could get.

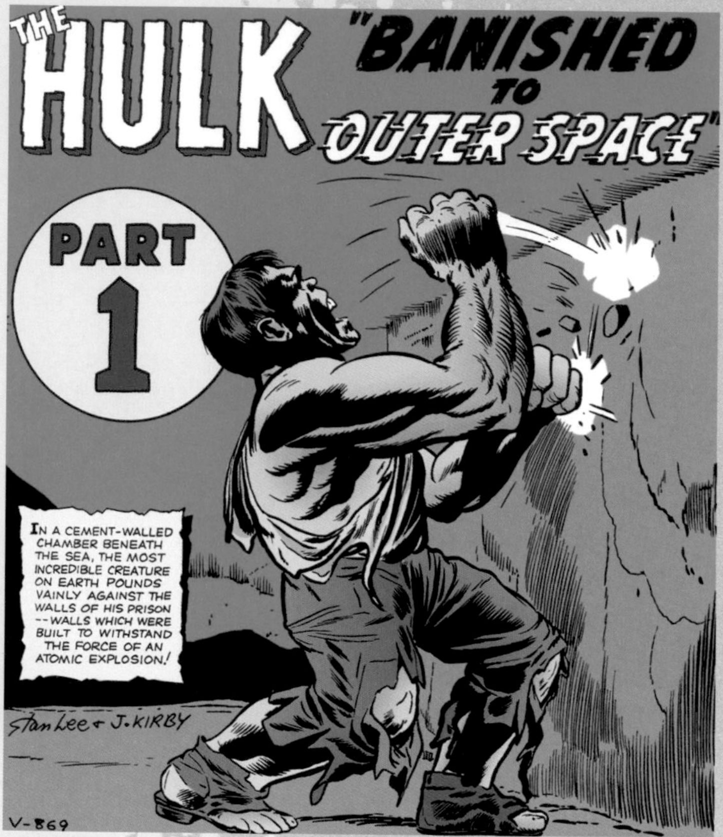
THE HULK
"BANISHED TO OUTER SPACE"
PART 1
IN A CEMENT-WALLED CHAMBER BENEATH THE SEA, THE MOST INCREDIBLE CREATURE ON EARTH POUNDS VAINLY AGAINST THE WALLS OF HIS PRISON --WALLS WHICH WERE BUILT TO WITHSTAND THE FORCE OF AN ATOMIC EXPLOSION!
Stan Lee + J. KIRBY
V-869

The Hulk started out with gray skin, but Marvel colorist Stan Goldberg argued that gray would not look good on the printed page. He convinced Stan Lee, and by the second issue, the Hulk was green.

The story of the Hulk began with a scientist named Bruce Banner. During a weapons experiment, Banner is exposed to massive doses of gamma gays. This radiation affects his body. At first, he transforms into the Hulk only after sunset. But soon the transformation is triggered any time by strong emotions, such as anger or jealousy. And the Hulk is not just Banner with extra powers. Banner is short and thin, but the Hulk is seven feet tall and weighs about one thousand pounds. He is strong, too—when angry, the Hulk can lift one hundred tons without breaking a sweat.

Aside from the Hulk's appearance, Lee and Kirby's story was different from ordinary superhero tales in other ways too. Most significantly,

Banner does not welcome his secret identity. He hates it. And once he transforms into the Hulk, he has no interest in saving humanity. The Hulk simply destroys stuff, fighting and getting revenge. In some ways, the Hulk was a complicated symbol for both good and evil. He was a reasonable scientist most of the time, but when threatened or hurt, he was roused to use enormous, uncontrollable power.

CLIMBING THE WALLS

Radiation was also behind Lee's next idea, a character called Spider-Man. Martin Goodman was discouraging. "He didn't want me to do it," Lee recalled years later. "He said I was way off base. He said, 'First of all, you can't call a hero Spider-Man, because people hate spiders.'" Goodman also objected to the fact that Spider-Man's alter ego, Peter Parker, was a teenager. Teenagers were not the heroes—they were the sidekicks. And finally, Goodman felt Lee was adding too many personal and family problems to Peter Parker's background story. Goodman told Lee to forget about Spider-Man.

But the story does not end there. One of Marvel's series was being canceled, and there was a last issue to fill. "When you're doing that last issue of a book," Lee explained, "nobody cares what you put into it, so—just to get it off my chest—I threw Spider-Man into that book and I featured him on the cover." Within a couple of months, the Spider-Man issue was Marvel's bestseller. Seeing the sales numbers, Goodman stopped by Lee's office and suggested that he do a series with "that Spider-Man character."

As with the Fantastic Four and the Hulk, Lee broke new ground with Peter Parker and Spider-Man. Characters such as Superman always did the right thing, and the pressures of everyday life never seemed to affect them. Clark Kent was an ordinary reporter making a modest income, but he never worried about paying the bills or saving up for a new car. Superman was an orphan ripped away from his family and his world. Yet he took the emotional upheaval in stride.

As a departure from type, Peter Parker's emotional troubles are woven into the Spider-Man stories.

Working with illustrator Steve Ditko, Lee set about creating a complex character that would connect with many young comic book readers. Peter is a shy high school student, uncomfortable with kids his own age. Orphaned as a boy, he lives a quiet life with his Aunt May and Uncle Ben. Life is quiet, that is, until Peter is bitten by a radioactive spider from a laboratory. He soon discovers that he has gained enormous strength and the ability to leap great distances, cling to walls, and maintain an extraordinary sense of balance. He also has a spider sense, a tingling sensation that warns him of danger.

Once Peter discovers his new abilities, he is more concerned with using them to make money than to do good. At one point, Peter is in a position to stop a burglar. But hoping to scoop

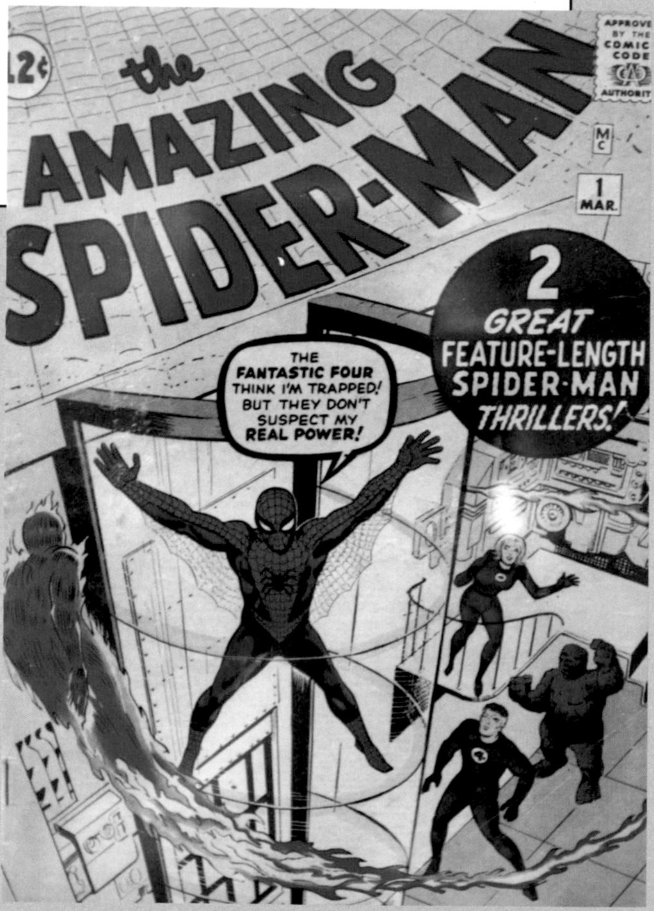
12¢
the AMAZING SPIDER-MAN
APPROVED BY THE COMIC CODE AUTHORITY
1 MAR.
2 GREAT FEATURE-LENGTH SPIDER-MAN THRILLERS!
THE FANTASTIC FOUR THINK I'M TRAPPED! BUT THEY DON'T SUSPECT MY REAL POWER!

Nobody likes spiders, and teenagers can't be superheroes. So Stan Lee was told when he floated the idea of Spider-Man to his publisher. Despite these concerns, Spider-Man made it into print as a minor character in 1962. Within a year, he had his own comic book.

up the burglar's stolen money, Peter lets him go. As the burglar runs away, he shoots Peter's Uncle Ben on the street. Peter realizes that his greed has led to a terrible consequence he did not foresee. As Ben dies in Peter's arms, Peter remembers something his uncle once said: "With great power there must also come great responsibility." And so Peter accepts his fate to become a crime-fighting superhero.

Lee gave Peter very human—and very teenage—flaws. And he placed the great lesson Peter must learn in the context of a family tragedy, making it easier for readers to relate to emotionally. These unique aspects of the Spider-Man story made him an instant hit.

The Hit Parade Continues

The Fantastic Four, the Incredible Hulk, and Spider-Man had secured Stan Lee's place in comic book history, but he was far from finished. Next up was Thor, a version of the ancient Norse god of thunder. Thor

12¢
JOURNEY INTO
MYSTERY
83 AUG.
INTRODUCING... THE MIGHTY THOR!
THE MOST EXCITING SUPER HERO OF ALL TIME!!
BEGIN THE SAGA OF THOR IN THIS ISSUE!

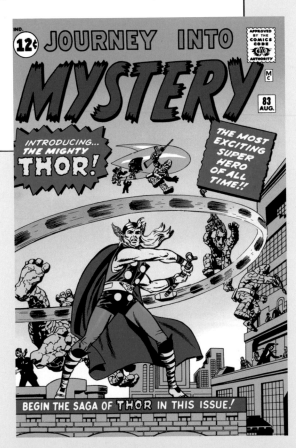

Thor first appeared in Marvel's *Journey into Mystery (right)* in 1962. Modeled after an ancient god revered by the Vikings, Thor wields a mighty hammer and wears a metal helmet.

starts out as Dr. Don Blake. Blake finds an ancient hammer hidden in a cave, and when he strikes it, he becomes the ancient Norse god. When Blake later failed to make a big enough impression with readers, it was explained that he was, in fact, Thor himself. However, his father, Odin, had punished his son by clouding his memory and putting his spirit in mortal form.

The X-Men didn't need any magic hammers to show their stuff. They were mutant human beings, each one born with a different power. Their leader was the telepathic Professor X, who ran a school for mutants to help them develop their powers and get along in the world.

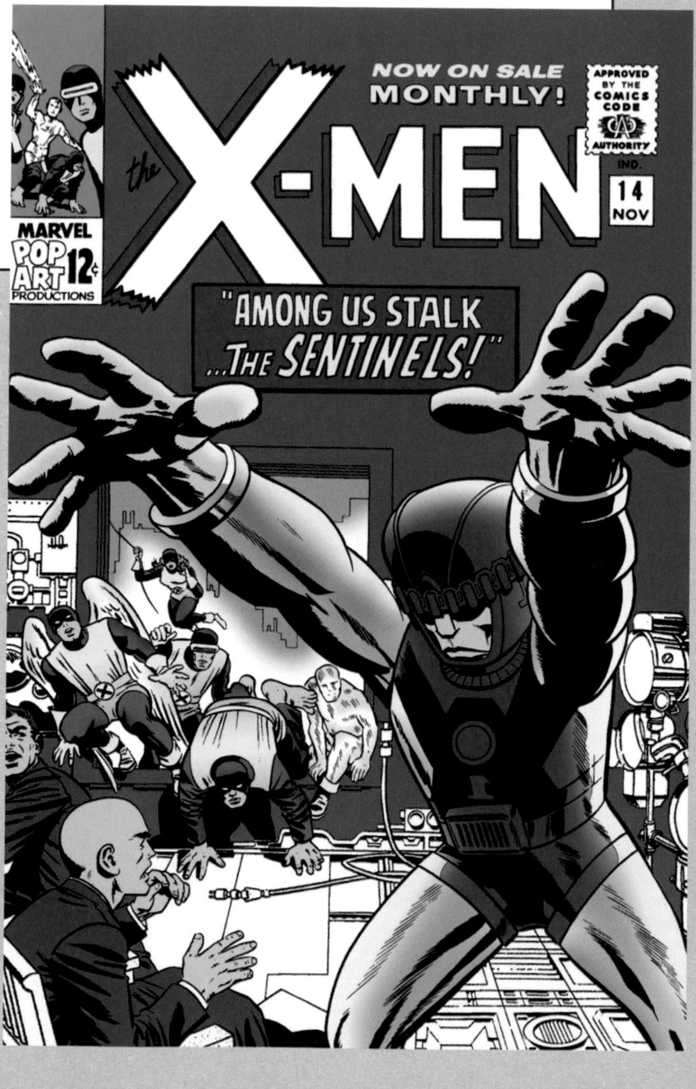
NOW ON SALE MONTHLY!
APPROVED BY THE COMICS CODE AUTHORITY
the X-MEN
IND. 14 NOV
MARVEL POP ART 12¢ PRODUCTIONS
"AMONG US STALK ...THE SENTINELS!"

The X-Men story began in 1963. In the first issues of the series *(right)*, Professor X gathered the original five mutants—Angel, Beast, Cyclops, Iceman, and Marvel Girl—at his school to teach them how to control their powers.

Dr. Strange had a different power, the power of magic.

Stan Lee developed other characters during this period. Daredevil, the man without fear, was the first blind superhero, but his other senses had been heightened to compensate. Iron Man was the alter ego of Tony Stark, who actually needed his armored technology to keep his damaged heart beating. And then there was the Silver Surfer, herald to the planet destroyer Galactus, left on Earth as punishment for betraying his master.

All of Lee's characters made the superhero universe crowded and diverse. Marvel Comics also started the idea of having stories from different heroes overlap with those in different issues. So readers who wanted to follow a particular plotline would sometimes have to buy comic books in a series they might not otherwise have chosen. It was a clever marketing strategy, but readers also genuinely enjoyed seeing their favorite superheroes interacting.

Clever story lines and interesting characters kept young readers coming back. Reader dedication to their favorite comic books seemed to contradict earlier fears about comics' negative influence. Instead of being a mindless waste of time, as critics had charged, comics seemed to spur an interest in reading in general. Teacher and writer Jeff Limke recalls his early childhood habit of reading every comic book available in the general store of his hometown in North Dakota. "I'm positive my love of books began there," Limke said. "As I got older, I read more and more novels, but I never left comics."

TIMES A-CHANGING

Superheroes were not the only comics on the scene in the early 1960s. The ever-growing influence of the youth culture drove clothing fashions, television programming, Hollywood movies, and the music industry. It also kept alive series such as Archie Comics.

Archie Comics are popular with younger readers looking forward to becoming teens. Mary Rodgers, a children's book editor from

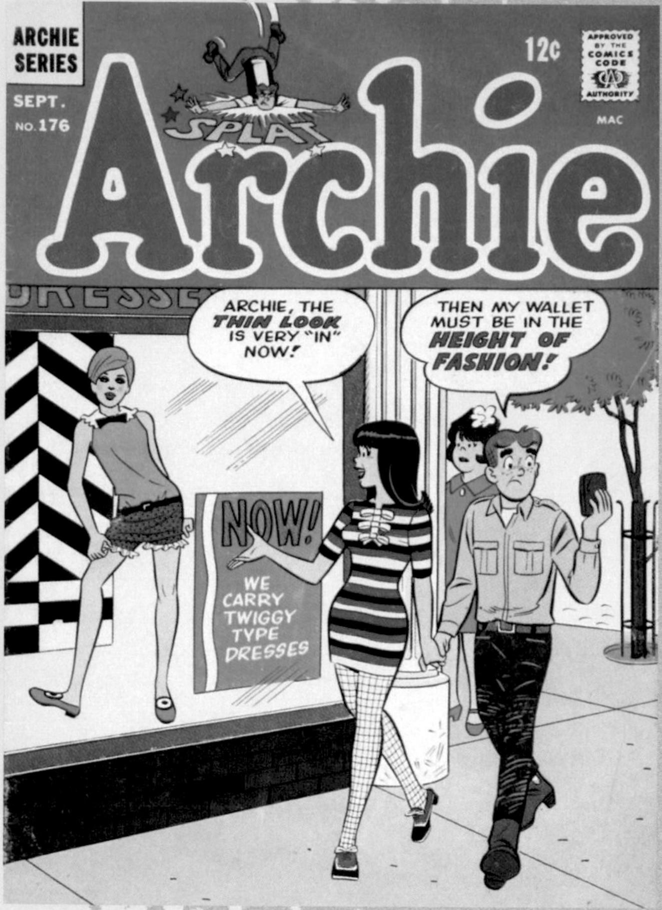
ARCHIE SERIES
SEPT. NO.176
12¢
APPROVED BY THE COMICS CODE AUTHORITY
MAC
Archie
SPLAT
ARCHIE, THE THIN LOOK IS VERY "IN" NOW!
THEN MY WALLET MUST BE IN THE HEIGHT OF FASHION!
NOW!
WE CARRY TWIGGY TYPE DRESSES

For decades, Archie Comics has reflected teenage styles and interests. In this 1967 issue *(left)*, Veronica enthuses over the "Twiggy look" on display in a store window. Twiggy (born Lesley Hornsby) is an English fashion model famous at the time for her thin figure and boyish haircut. Fashions from Great Britain were very popular in the United States during the 1960s.

Minneapolis, recalls comic books as "the preferred summer reading among my siblings and friends." Rodgers's extended family shared a summer cabin on the Russian River in northern California, and the Rodgers kids would read comics while lounging on the beach beside the river. "My brothers and I each got money to buy a few comics. We made a special effort not to duplicate purchases, so we could trade throughout the summer. The Archie Comics were our favorite. I think it was the boy-girl interplay we enjoyed."

The Archie stories stayed simple, and the characters were always squeaky clean. Still, Archie Comics tried to reflect, in its own way, the changing youth culture. In the 1950s, cotton shirts, long skirts for girls, and dress pants for boys were common clothes. But by the early 1960s, teen clothes were brighter and more unusual, reflecting artsy influences such as the mod movement in Great Britain. Archie, Jughead, Veronica, and the rest of the "gang" joined the trend, dressing in fringed jackets, brightly colored shirts, miniskirts, and bell-bottom jeans. The Archies still annoyed their teachers and fretted about prom dates. But they also sang folk songs and went on protest marches against racial discrimination and sexism, as real-life youth were starting to do. In this era, Archie Comics was popular enough to produce two spin-offs—minor characters who ended up getting their own comic books. Sabrina the Teenaged Witch appeared in 1962, followed the next year by the all-girl rock band Josie and the Pussycats.

Whether humanizing their superheroes or restyling their teen stars, comic books tried to keep up with the times. But they would soon discover that the changes were only beginning.

Keep on Truckin'...
TRUCKIN' ON DOWN THE LINE...
HEY HEY HEY...
I SAID KEEP ON TRUCKIN'...
TRUCKIN' MY BLUES AWAY!

"Keep on Truckin'" by R. Crumb was originally drawn in 1968, but was reproduced on merchandise throughout the 1970s. Originally the title of a blues song, "keep on truckin'" became a catchphrase for a relaxed, laid-back attitude.

GOING UNDERGROUND

> **Keep on truckin'...**
>
> *—R. Crumb poster from 1968*

The late 1960s and early 1970s were times of great unrest in the United States. The generation that had proudly survived the depression and triumphed in World War II seemed to their children to be out of step with social changes. The younger generation thought their parents were too set in their ways. They were boring and traditional. And they were far too willing to follow authority figures without question. The phrase "generation gap" described this gulf between parents and children.

The Vietnam War, a conflict between Communist North Vietnam and non-Communist South Vietnam, had begun in the 1950s. By the 1960s, it was a hot-button issue in the United States. The older generation seemed to accept the U.S. government's argument that the Vietnam conflict was necessary to stop the spread of Communism. But much of the younger generation believed the U.S. government was sending American soldiers to die in a useless war.

Any authority figure or any part of the governing powers—known as the establishment—came under youthful suspicion in this era. "Don't trust anyone over thirty!" was one rallying cry. This suspicion even extended to Superman or Batman. These characters never aged on the printed page, but they had been around for decades. Their attitudes and story lines seemed hopelessly old fashioned. As the 1960s wore on, even Spider-Man seemed to be part of the ruling structure. Comic book heroes might be troubled, they might have human problems, but they were still viewed by some young readers as part of the establishment.

THE GROWING GAP

Most prominent comics publishers stayed out of the Vietnam War issue. Spider-Man had a friend who went off to fight. And Iron Man, who in his real-life identity as Tony Stark had invented many weapons, questioned what those weapons were being used for. But most publishers avoided the war as a topic for practical reasons. No matter which side the stories took, publishers feared losing sales.

For the same reason, many publishers also shied away from other serious social issues of the time. African Americans, women, and gay and lesbian people were all fighting for fair and equal treatment on the job, in education, and in their everyday lives. They fought against stereotypes that portrayed them as untrustworthy, weak, unintelligent, and even mentally ill. For much of mainstream America, these civil rights battles were unnerving. They threatened the status quo—the comfortable, familiar way of doing things. Mainstream comics publishers abandoned some of the most offensive racial and sexual stereotypes, but many were unwilling to tackle any real controversy that might upset readers.

Another difficult social issue comic book publishers could not delve into was the growing drug subculture. The comics code prevented publishers from treating any crime, including illegal drug use, as glamorous or interesting. Drug users, it was believed, were always sad characters living on the edge of society. But during the 1960s, some young Americans—even educated kids from middle-class families—began experimenting with drugs such as marijuana and LSD (also known as acid). They believed that drugs intensify a person's senses, memories, and emotions. Drugs would expand their

During the 1960s, many young people sought to distinguish their political and social attitudes from those of their parents. Calling themselves hippies (from *hip*, meaning up-to-date on trends), many also dressed distinctively, with colorful clothes and long hair.

consciousness—that is, loosen their inhibitions and heighten their senses. In fact, the common experiences of a drug "trip"—vivid colors, swirling or fractured patterns, distorted sounds, and rambling speech—became part of a cultural trend. Called psychedelia, the colors and sounds were echoed in everything from fabric design to music. But comic books could not examine this drug use trend as anything other than an old-fashioned law-and-order issue.

The Comics Code Is Broken

By the late 1960s and early 1970s, comic book publishers were willing to take risks, however. Stan Lee and Marvel proposed a three-part Spider-Man story warning kids about the dangers of drug addiction. The story hoped to point out that drug use, however trendy, was still harmful. The CCA refused to approve the story despite its good intentions. Marvel decided that the issue was too important to ignore—and published it anyway. So what happened? The sky did not fall, and the strong sales showed that the CCA stamp was no longer as powerful as it once had been.

Raising the fictional stakes on Marvel's drug story, DC's Green Arrow discovers that his sidekick Speedy has a drug addiction. Speedy beats the addiction over time, and the success of every issue further challenged the CCA—which did not approve of these themes even in a good cause.

DC was also increasing its spotlight on social problems. A 1970 issue of *Green Lantern* featured the hero rescuing a man being attacked by a kid. This seems to be a straightforward situation until Green Arrow steps in. He explains to the Green Lantern that the man is actually a slum landlord—a building owner who rents run-down apartments to poor people. The slum landlord wants to tear down an apartment building, leaving its residents without a home. The kid is trying to stop him. The theme was preachy and not especially subtle, but it was a long way from a fight with an intergalactic villain.

Moving in New Directions

Just as mainstream comic book publishers were testing the comics code, a comics subculture decided to completely undermine the code. In the late 1960s, underground comics operating under the radar of the CCA emerged. Most underground comic book publishers were small operations, often run out of someone's apartment or basement. Their readers were older—high school and college students who had grown up reading traditional comics. They still wanted to read comics, but they wanted something more, something different and edgier. Underground comics became known as comix to distinguish them further from traditional comics.

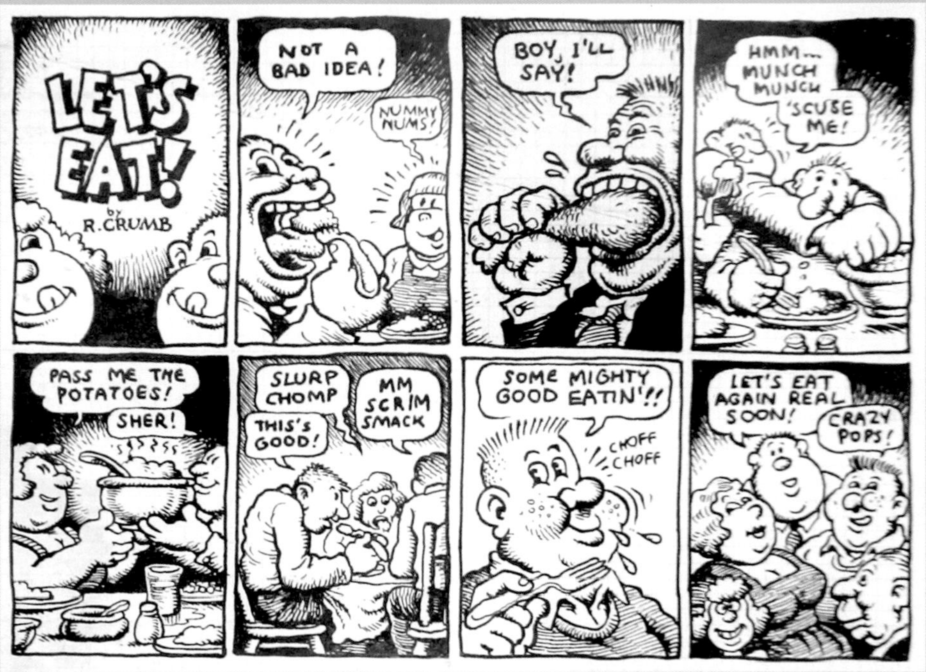
LET'S EAT!
by R. CRUMB
NOT A BAD IDEA!
NUMMY NUMS!
BOY, I'LL SAY!
HMM... MUNCH MUNCH
'SCUSE ME!
PASS ME THE POTATOES!
SHER!
SLURP CHOMP
MM SCRIM SMACK
THIS'S GOOD!
SOME MIGHTY GOOD EATIN'!!
CHOFF CHOFF
LET'S EAT AGAIN REAL SOON!
CRAZY POPS!

R. Crumb used his comics to poke fun at aspects of American life. "Let's Eat" features a fat family centering all their attention on their food.

In embracing the fringes of youth culture, including psychedelia, comix emphasized sex, drugs, and rock 'n' roll. The comix were not like those of mainstream companies such as DC and Marvel, which only occasionally touched on drugs and other risky behavior. For comix publishers, drugs and risky behavior were good things. Comix themes and attitudes appealed to the growing and mostly young counterculture, a movement dedicated to radical politics and to freedom from the conventional life of marriage and steady jobs.

The most famous of the comix creators was Robert Crumb, known as R. Crumb. Crumb began his career as an illustrator in Cleveland, Ohio, and in New York City. In 1967 he moved to San Francisco, California—then the center of American counterculture. He began Zap Comix in 1968 to publish his own ideas and artwork.

Crumb's style reflects humorous cartoon styles from the 1920s and 1930s. It also suggests some of the visual distortion of psychedelic drug use. Characters usually have at least one enormously exaggerated feature—a huge nose, gigantic feet, or bloated hands. The scratchy ink strokes of his shading and detail give his cartoons a purposely shabby look. And his stories usually involve sex and a drug-altered view of the world—popular counterculture themes.

Not everyone in the counterculture, however, admired Crumb. Some feminists (people who support equal rights for women) found Crumb's work degrading to women. His female characters are often depicted in humiliating or violent sexual situations. Others found Crumb's work offensive to African Americans and other minorities, who are sometimes depicted with stereotypical facial features. Crumb also occasionally used insulting racial terms in his dialogue. Crumb has since apologized for some offenses. In other cases, he has argued that readers are missing the point. He claims that he is actually ridiculing racism in his work.

Despite such controversies, underground comics actually provided a forum for a more diverse group of writers and artists. In 1970 two women, Trina Robbins and Willy Mendes, moved to San Francisco to be a part of the growing underground scene. Feeling excluded by some of the all-male comix operations, Robbins and Mendes started their own feminist newspaper, *It Ain't Me, Babe*, which included Robbins's comic strips. Robbins, Mendes, and a few other women then established *It Ain't Me, Babe Comics*. They also began gathering comix from other feminist writers and artists, including Aline Kominsky, who would later marry R. Crumb. Robbins and Mendes published the feminist work in a continuing collection called *Wimmen's Comix*. At a time when mainstream comics were dominated by superheroes and teenage comedy, feminist comix looked at topics such as discrimination against women, female sexuality and body image, and lesbian relationships.

As women made their mark in the underground, minorities gained some ground in mainstream comic books. Outside the mainstream,

BUT, BEFORE THE MAD MASTER OF SOUND CAN ACTIVATE HIS STRANGE WEAPON, THE BLACK PANTHER, MOVING AS SWIFTLY AS HIS NAMESAKE, HURLS THE FATAL POWER SWITCH WHICH HIS NIMBLE FINGERS HAD BEEN SILENTLY GROPING FOR--!
MY CONVERTER! IT-IT'S BEING BLOWN APART!!
IT HAS TO END THIS WAY-- IN THE NAME OF JUSTICE!
YOU DID NOT REALIZE-- I AM A SCIENTIST, TOO--!
THUS, I COULD TELL WHICH LEVER TO THROW IN ORDER TO OVERLOAD YOUR DELICATE ELECTRONIC CIRCUITS!
AND NOW, ONLY MY PANTHER SPEED CAN SAVE ME FROM THE HOLOCAUST WHICH IS ABOUT TO BEFALL--!
IT'S OVER! THE CAVE IS DESTROYED! NEVERMORE SHALL THE MASTER OF SOUND'S UNCANNY MONSTERS THREATEN MY LAND!
MAY YOUR ETERNAL SLEEP BE A PEACEFUL ONE, T'CHAKA MY FATHER!! THIS DAY YOU HAVE BEEN AVENGED!
AT THAT MOMENT, THOUSANDS OF YARDS AWAY, FIVE PAIR OF STARTLED EYES SEE THE ELECTRIFYING UPHEAVAL--
THAT ENTIRE HILL--IT'S BEEN SHATTERED INTO NOTHING-NESS!
WHAT IS IT, REED? WHAT DOES IT MEAN?
I'M NOT SURE, JOHNNY--BUT I HAVE A FEELING THAT THE BLACK PANTHER IS SOMEHOW RESPONSIBLE!
THE SOUND IS DEAFENING!! IT'S LIKE THE END OF THE WORLD! HOLD ME, MY DARLING--!
HEY! LOOK--OVER THERE! A COUPLE MORE OF THEM REFUGEES FROM GOD-ZILLA!
BUT--THEY'RE FADING AWAY!! THEY MUST SOMEHOW BE LINKED TO THE EXPLOSION!
WHATEVER IT WAS THAT HAS BEEN DESTROYED, MUST HAVE BEEN THE THING THAT CREATED THEM!
19

In this 1966 comic book, the Black Panther helps the Fantastic Four defeat a villain named Klaw. The Black Panthers were also a radical African American political group of the 1960s and 1970s, but Marvel's Black Panther was not named after the group.

African American publications such as the *Chicago Defender* had long published strips written and drawn by African Americans and featuring African American heroes and characters. The civil rights movement and political activism of the 1960s and 1970s encouraged mainstream comic book publishers to include minority characters. For example, the first African American superhero, the Black Panther, joined the Fantastic Four in the late 1960s. At the same time, Brumsic Brandon Jr. introduced an entire cast of

By the 1970s, Will Eisner had been in the comic book business for three decades. He began looking for alternatives to traditional comic book themes.

working-class African American kids in *Luther*. And in 1972, Luke Cage was the first African American superhero to get his own self-titled comic book, published by Marvel.

These comics dealt realistically with racial issues and life in minority communities. And comic book publishers were becoming more sensitive to racial stereotyping in characters' physical appearance. But these new minority characters were often pigeonholed in other ways. African American characters were often strongly political, had hot tempers, or spoke in a "ghetto" dialect. Asian characters almost always practiced martial arts such as karate or ninjutsu. And Native American heroes were often mysterious and mystically spiritual. Certainly, the range of comic books was expanding, but it still had a way to go in creating a truly diverse community of characters.

GRAPHIC NOVELS

While many comic book publishers worked on taking characters and attitudes in a new direction, Will Eisner worked on taking the comic book format to a new level. By the 1970s, Eisner was no longer interested in the traditional comic book story lines he had helped pioneer thirty years earlier. Eisner wanted to use the comic book art form—illustrated panels or "sequential art," as he called it—to tell longer and more complex stories. And to distinguish these stories from heroic fantasies or goofy cartoon adventures, Eisner used the term *graphic novel*.

The term had appeared as far back as the 1950s. Eisner remembers using it in a particular 1978 phone conversation with a New York book publisher. Eisner was trying to interest the publisher in a newly finished work. He felt the publisher would not take him seriously if he called his new work a comic book. "There's something I want to show you . . . ," Eisner recalls telling the publisher. "He said, 'Yeah, well, what is it?' A little man in my head popped up and said, 'Don't tell him it's a comic. He'll hang up on you.' So I said, 'It's a graphic novel.' He said, 'Wow! That sounds interesting.'"

The 1978 work in question was *A Contract with God*. The book is a collection of four stories set in the Bronx, New York, during the Great Depression. The characters live in a tenement (a run-down apartment building often rented to poor immigrants). Eisner drew on his own experiences growing up in an impoverished but close-knit Jewish neighborhood. The stories reveal how the people deal with death and poverty and how they look for a better life. There are no gimmicks—no costumes, superheroes, slam-bang action, or slapstick antics. Instead, Eisner uses realistic storytelling to focus closely on the emotional lives of ordinary people.

The critical acclaim *A Contract with God* received suggested to many mainstream readers that comic books were more than mindless entertainment. Eisner's work showed that the comic book format could grow as an art form by taking on more complicated topics at greater length. It was another sign that the boundaries of the comic book were expanding again.

MATT GROENING

On the TV cartoon show *The Simpsons*, Comic Book Guy is the owner of the Android's Dungeon & Baseball Card Shop. Known for his bad attitude toward customers and his obsession with sci-fi trivia, Comic Book Guy pokes fun at the stereotype of a socially inept comic book fan.

LOOKING FORWARD AND BACK

Bart: Well, between us we've read all 814 issues of Radioactive Man.
Milhouse: Yeah, and we both have the special limited edition issue where he and Fallout Boy get killed on every page.

—*Bart Simpson and Milhouse van Houten, discussing their favorite comic book hero at the Android's Dungeon & Baseball Card Shop*, The Simpsons, *September 1995*

A *Contract with God* had set the stage for a new artistic trend in comic book publishing. For the true comic book fan, this trend, along with traditional comics and increasing imports from Japan and other countries, offered even more reading choices.

But the early 1980s were tough times for comic book sales. The world of pop culture was expanding in several new directions. Arcade video games had become quite popular, introducing an interactive element to fantasy stories. Why read about spaceships blowing up or watch them blow up, when you could be doing the blowing up yourself? Of course, if you did choose to watch a science fiction or fantasy movie, improved special effects made movies such as the Star Wars series or *Raiders of the Lost Ark* thrilling experiences. Rock and pop music fans were drawn into MTV, an entire television channel devoted to the new medium of music videos. In contrast, comic books were still just words and pictures, pretty tame in the exploding world of new media.

As a result, publishers began including new gimmicks in the hope of spurring sales and maintaining reader interest. Some covers included holograms (a special photographic 3-D image). Others glowed in the dark. The same story would even be published in special issues with several different covers to prompt devoted fans to buy them all.

The Comics Shop

The comic book industry was feeling added pressure as traditional outlets for comic books sales, such as newsstands, independently owned drugstores, and small corner grocery stores, began to disappear. The loss of traditional outlets for comic books affected buyers as well as publishers. Comic book fans began to look for new places to shop. Their searches led to the rapid growth of comics shops in the 1980s.

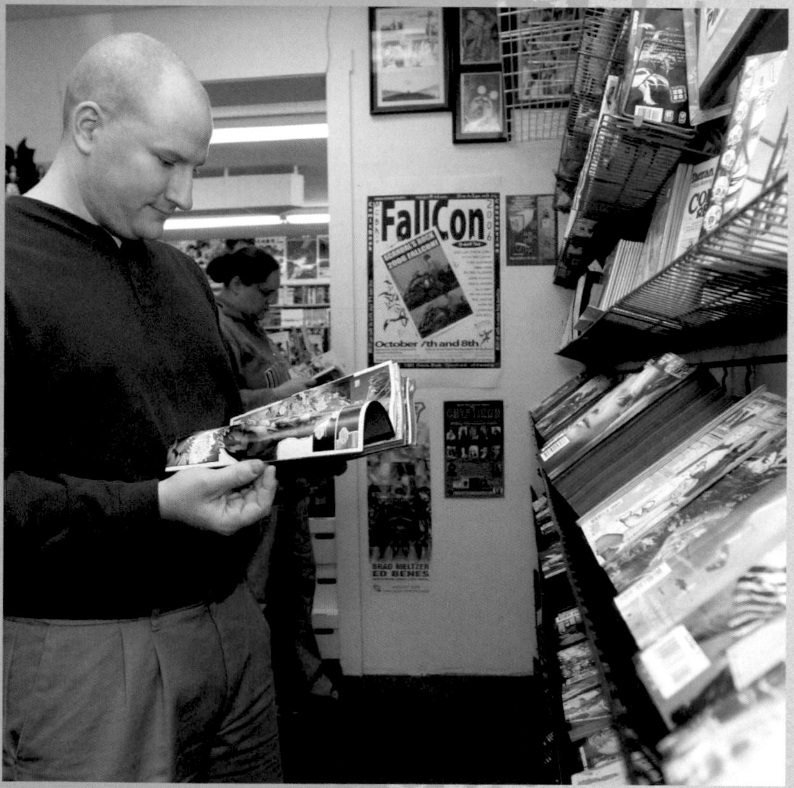
FallCon
October 7th and 8th

A customer looks through comic books in a comics shop. Many comic book shops sell back issues—copies of previously published comic books—as well as current issues.

Comic shops are bookstores, often small and independently owned, that specialize in all kinds of comic books and graphic novels. Many carry back issues (issues no longer in print), special issues, rare comics, and manga (Japanese comics). Some also carry related items such as action figures, posters, and anime (animated films from Japan). For comic book fans, the comics shop is a treasure house.

But the shops play another important role for fans—they provide a place for comic book lovers to meet. In the 1980s, some people still looked down on comic books and their readers. Young adult comic book fans felt self-conscious about their interest. Comics shops provided a place for them to meet other people who followed the history, story lines, and character development of their favorite series.

Brian Miller, a digital painter and comic book colorist from Phoenix, Arizona, believes a well-run comics shop is important to serious readers. "The best shops learn how to get the little things right to make shopping there fun. If I read *Buffy the Vampire Slayer*, the store staff might recommend a vampire book from another publisher I'm not aware of, or they might recommend an X-Men book written by Buffy creator Joss Whedon."

Comics shops became so common that *The Simpsons*, the long-running animated TV show, features the Android's Dungeon & Baseball Card Shop. Its owner, known only as Comic Book Guy, is an amusing stereotype of an obsessive science fiction and fantasy fan. But despite Comic Book Guy's hostility and nerdiness, his shop is where Bart Simpson and all his friends gather to buy their comic books.

DUDES AND 'TUDES

As fans found new places to buy comic books, aspiring writers and artists tried to come up with fresh ideas, both serious and funny, to interest them. In many cases, publishers were most interested in comic book series that could also be developed as TV shows or as a line of action figures.

EASTMAN AND LAIRD'S
TALES OF THE
TEENAGE MUTANT NINJA
TURTLES
NO. 2
$1.50
JULY

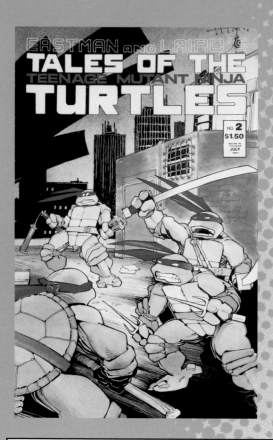

Teenage Mutant Ninja Turtles was based on some fairly worn-out comic book fads, such as mutant-producing accidents and mysterious martial arts experts. But creators Eastman and Laird's sense of fun and the turtles' teenage attitudes made the series popular.

One series that fit the bill perfectly is about four crime fighters living deep in the heart of New York City's sewers. The Teenage Mutant Ninja Turtles were the 1984 creation of two young freelance illustrators from Massachusetts, Kevin Eastman and Peter Laird. They created and produced their new comic book series without the support of a major publishing house.

The story of the Ninjas begins when four normal turtles fall through an open manhole cover on a New York City street. They land in some mysterious goo and find themselves mutating, or transforming, over the next few days. They grow huge, begin to walk on two feet, and learn to talk. A sewer rat named Splinter takes the mutated turtles under his wing and teaches them martial arts. He also gives them each a name from an old book he finds about Italian Renaissance painters of the fifteenth and sixteenth centuries: Leonardo, Raphael, Michelangelo, and Donatello.

The Teenage Mutant Ninja Turtles fight as a team, but each has a distinct personality. The four turtles hone their skills fighting bad guys, but they were meant, in part at least, to spoof regular superheroes. The series became enormously popular, and action figures and a Saturday morning television cartoon show soon followed.

A Revolution at DC

To keep up with new and fresh comic book ideas, large publishers reenergized some of their well-established characters. Writer and artist Frank Miller had already taken Marvel's Spider-Man and Daredevil into darker territory. DC asked him to do the same for them. In 1986 he created *Batman: The Dark Knight Returns*. This story is set in the not-too-distant future where a middle-aged Batman comes out of retirement to fight a gang called the Mutants. But the fighting does not stop there. The Joker is on the rampage, but there is nothing funny about the murders he is committing. Batman must also fight Superman because the government wants Batman to stop taking justice into his own hands. (The fight will be fairer than you might think because a nuclear explosion has blocked out the sun, depriving Superman of most of his powers.) *The Dark Knight Returns* was a hit. It was stark and powerful, increasing the mystery surrounding a pop culture icon. Batman was back.

Another example of DC's efforts to stretch itself came with Alan Moore's twelve-part *Watchmen* series, first published in 1986. The Watchmen exist in a world parallel to our own, where the Soviet Union and the United States are threatening nuclear war against each other. Against this backdrop, members of a retired group of superheroes are being murdered. At the heart of this mystery is Ozymandias, also known as Adrian Veidt, a former crime fighter who has become the world's richest man. Critics and readers hailed the series for its visual look. Dramatic close-ups pulled the reader into the story. The series was written for adults rather than children, and it later won the prestigious science fiction Hugo Award.

THE MOUSE THAT ROARED

Art Spiegelman's *Maus*, a graphic novel first published in 1986, also appealed to older readers, but it contained an important message for young readers. *Maus* tells the story of Spiegelman's father, a Polish Jew imprisoned in a Nazi concentration camp during World War II. The action is realistic, but Spiegelman adds an allegorical touch. In *Maus*, the characters have human bodies but animal heads. The Jews are mice (*maus* is German for "mouse"), and the Nazis are cats.

Maus is a remarkable novel. The Holocaust, the relentless extermination of Jews by the Nazis during World War II, is a serious, solemn historical event. Yet Spiegelman chose to tell this story, so close to his own heart, in the comic book format. "*Maus* was done in comics form because I make comics," he explained, "and so it was the natural language for me to speak. Comics have to do with art like Yiddish [a German-Hebrew dialect spoken by Jews] has to do with language; it's a kind of vernacular [an everyday language common to a community]."

Another moody and dramatic debut was Neil Gaiman's *The Sandman* in 1989. Otherwise known as Morpheus, the title character is the God of the Dreamworld. His siblings included Death, Destiny, Delirium, and Despair. *The Sandman* is a complex, absorbing story, combining elements of fantasy, horror, and classical mythology. DC Comics was so impressed with *The Sandman* that it made the book the first publication in its Vertigo imprint (a publishing brand name). The series continued for seventy-five issues. "*The Sandman* series really got under my skin," recalls Justine Fontes, a graphic novelist from Readfield, Maine. "Death, Dream, Delirium, and the other

Maus is based on the stories Art Spiegelman's father, Vladek, told about life in Nazi-occupied Poland during World War II. Vladek survived imprisonment at Auschwitz, one of the most notorious Nazi concentration camps.

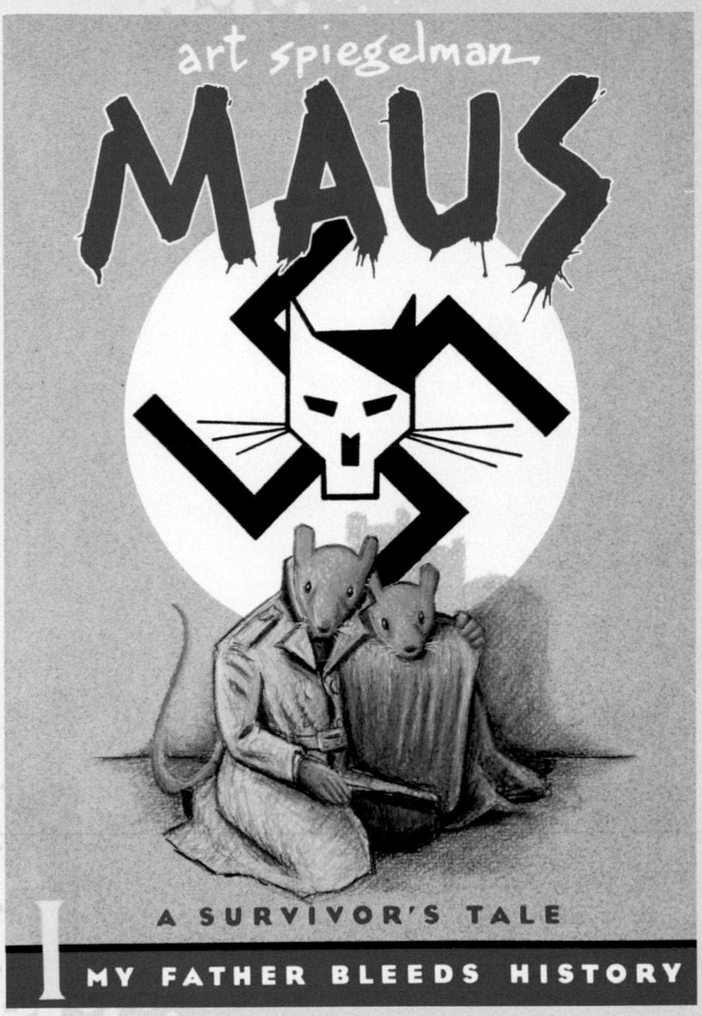
art spiegelman
MAUS
A SURVIVOR'S TALE
I MY FATHER BLEEDS HISTORY

Immortals feel both mythological and modern. The stories are real stories, not just fights in tights."

The success of graphic novels such as *Maus* and *The Sandman* inspired other graphic novelists to tackle history, mythology, politics, and cultural issues. The increasingly popular manga, with its use of Japanese fantasy and mythology, was also influential. These subjects lent a new weight to graphic novels. They drew the attention of an older and more literary audience. And they held the interest of traditional comic book readers as well.

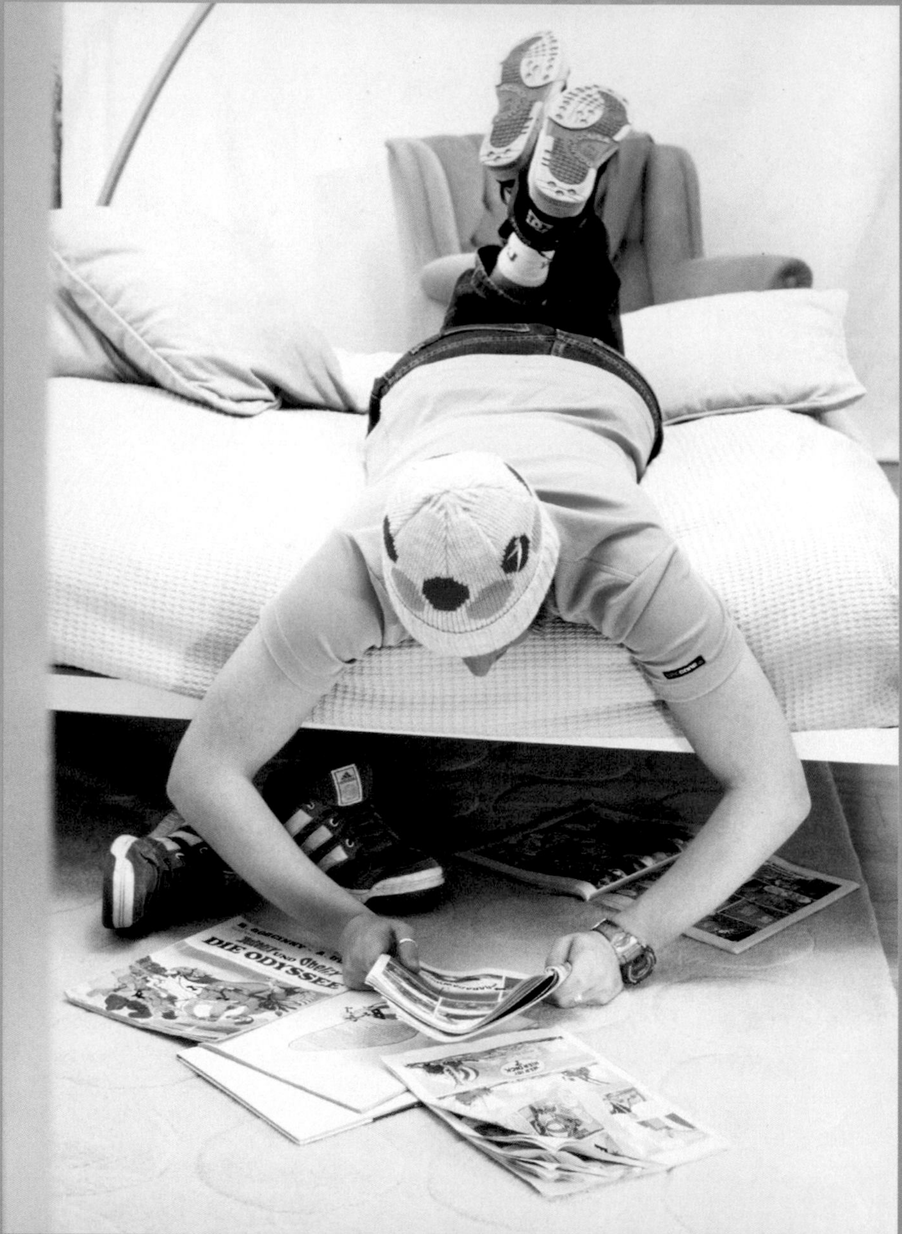
DIE ODYSSEE

A comic book fan relaxes with some of the latest issues. For many fans, following on-going story lines becomes a kind of hobby.

The World Turned Upside Down

> **Comic books are like potato chips—fans cannot have just one.**
>
> —*Matthew J. Pustz,* Comic Book Culture, *1999*

While comic books changed from within in the late twentieth century, the biggest influences on the industry were coming from outside the publishing world. In 1989 the Berlin Wall, which had separated Soviet-controlled East Berlin and democratic West Berlin since the 1960s, was torn down. The wall was a powerful symbol of repressive Communism. Its destruction was a sign of momentous things to come. Two years later, the Soviet Union peacefully ended. The Cold War melted away. War itself had not been eliminated, but humanity seemed to have taken a couple of steps back from various doomsday scenarios.

A Death in the Family

With global annihilation unlikely for the moment, comic book publishers took a hard look at other themes to develop to keep their readership. In 1991 DC Comics came up with a radical idea—to kill off one of the oldest and best-loved characters in the comic book universe.

"We have these big Superman meetings," explains DC editor Mike Carlin, "with every writer and artist, even the colorists. We all go into a room and just throw out ideas. And at every single meeting, as a joke,

FUNERAL FOR A FRIEND/1
THE ADVENTURES OF
SUPERMAN
498
WORLD WITHOUT A SUPERMAN!
BY ORDWAY, GRUMMETT & HAZLEWOOD

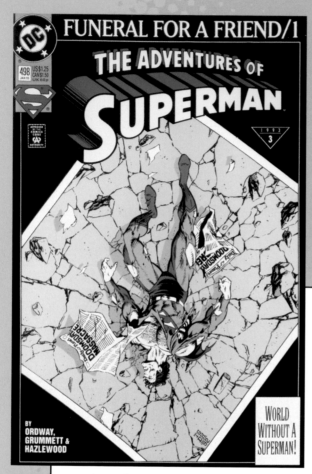

Superman's death created a media sensation. He wasn't the first superhero to die, but he was the most famous. By 1993 Superman had been part of the comic book world for sixty years. Fans were shocked to learn that he had been killed.

somebody has said 'Let's kill him!' It never failed—then we actually did it."

The story of Superman's death culminated in *Superman* #75 in January 1993. And who was Superman's killer? It was a monster named Doomsday that was crossing the country destroying everything in its path. Superman confronts it in Metropolis, and theirs is truly a fight to the death.

Superheroes had been killed before, but Superman stood alone. Word of his impending demise was front-page news across the country. Even more noteworthy, some of the people who mourned the loss of Superman did not read the Superman comic books—and maybe never had. He was so woven into the fabric of American life that announcing his death was like announcing the death of apple pie.

Even DC had not expected such a strong reaction. But once it began, the company took full advantage of all the attention. DC put out special editions of the comic and followed with lavish details of Superman's funeral (all of the DC superheroes naturally attended).

Yet profitable superheroes never stay dead for long. In Superman's case, it was discovered that his coffin actually was empty. DC's editors were in no hurry to bring him back too fast. They unveiled several different Superman successors before resurrecting America's most famous superhero in the fall of 1993.

Speculating on the Future

Maintaining fresh episodes is difficult with any ongoing story line—especially one that stretches over years or even decades. Some comic book fans saw the death of Superman as a daring story twist. Being willing to take a risk with a character such as Superman was one way to keep the story fresh and to create a buzz among readers.

Other readers criticized Superman's death as a gimmick or a publicity stunt. They saw it as a hyped-up special edition. Publishers had been using special editions to spur sales for years. People collected the special editions and different versions of comic books as investments, hoping they would become collector's items. Collectors could then resell them later at a much higher price. The practice helped fuel a market among speculators—buyers who take a risk that something will increase in value.

The special edition fad did actually greatly increase sales for a while. Eager to cash in on this market, comic book publishers had also added other products to their collectible lines, such as action figures and trading cards. But collector's items only become valuable when their numbers are limited. Comic book publishers in the 1990s made the mistake of flooding the market with special editions and merchandise. The comic books and toys were not rare enough to increase in value. So demand for special editions fell off, and collectors who had spent thousands on them quickly began selling off their copies. The comics speculation boom went bust.

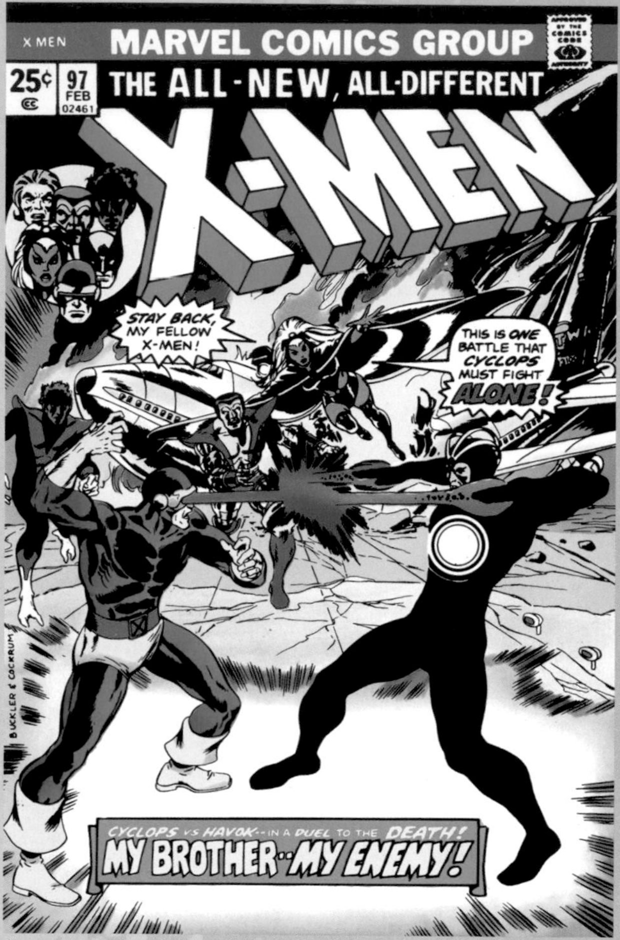
X MEN
MARVEL COMICS GROUP
25¢ 97 FEB
THE ALL-NEW, ALL-DIFFERENT
X-MEN
STAY BACK, MY FELLOW X-MEN!
THIS IS ONE BATTLE THAT CYCLOPS MUST FIGHT ALONE!
CYCLOPS VS HAVOK--IN A DUEL TO THE DEATH!
MY BROTHER--MY ENEMY!
BUCKLER & COCKRUM

Even popular series such as X-Men suffered during the lagging sales of the late 1980s and early 1990s.

For longtime comics fans, speculation only seemed to drive up the price of comic books and drive down the quality. Publishers appeared more absorbed in releasing special editions quickly than in creating interesting stories and art. Many fans felt that the comic book industry had become too corporate, only concerned with profits.

Dwindling sales, the speculation crash, and a few other bad business choices endangered even the largest comic book publishers. In 1996 Marvel—unable to meet the financial demands of running the company—declared bankruptcy. As it reorganized its finances, Marvel was forced to reduce all of its publishing plans, even those involving its highly successful X-Men series.

New Publishers Take the Stands

Even in the face of lagging sales, comic book publishing found new ways to reinvent itself. As some of the publishing giants struggled, new, smaller publishers found a foothold in the business. Smaller, independent comic book publishers were not unknown. For example, Dark Horse Comics, founded by Mike Richardson in the 1980s, had already published *Concrete*, *Aliens*, *Predator*, and other popular titles. But in the 1990s, more independent-minded artists and writers decided to strike out on their own, forming several small comic book publishing companies.

Among them was Todd McFarlane, who created Spawn for Image Comics. Spawn is not a happy well-adjusted character. A former CIA assassin in life, he has made a deal with a demon in hell to return to Earth to see his wife. However, he refuses to help the demon destroy heaven, and so the forces of both heaven and hell line up against him. Luckily, he has a number of useful powers including flight, super-strength, and a shape-changing ability. This may not be enough to ensure a happy ending, but it does improve the odds of his survival.

In 1993 Dark Horse Comics dipped into the world of demons with *Hellboy*. Hellboy is a demon summoned to Earth during a secret Nazi ritual in the last days of World War II. Rescued by the Allies, Hellboy grows up large and red, with horns and a pointy tail. He's not particularly cheerful, but he's not evil. He uses his supernatural powers to help the Bureau of Paranormal Research and Defense search out monsters, werewolves, vampires, and ghosts.

Dark Horse scored another hit in 1993 with *Sin City*. Sin City is the nickname for Basin City, a cesspool of corrupt politicians, businesspeople, and religious leaders. Crime fighters there commit crimes as often as they fight them, leaving ordinary people with a lot to

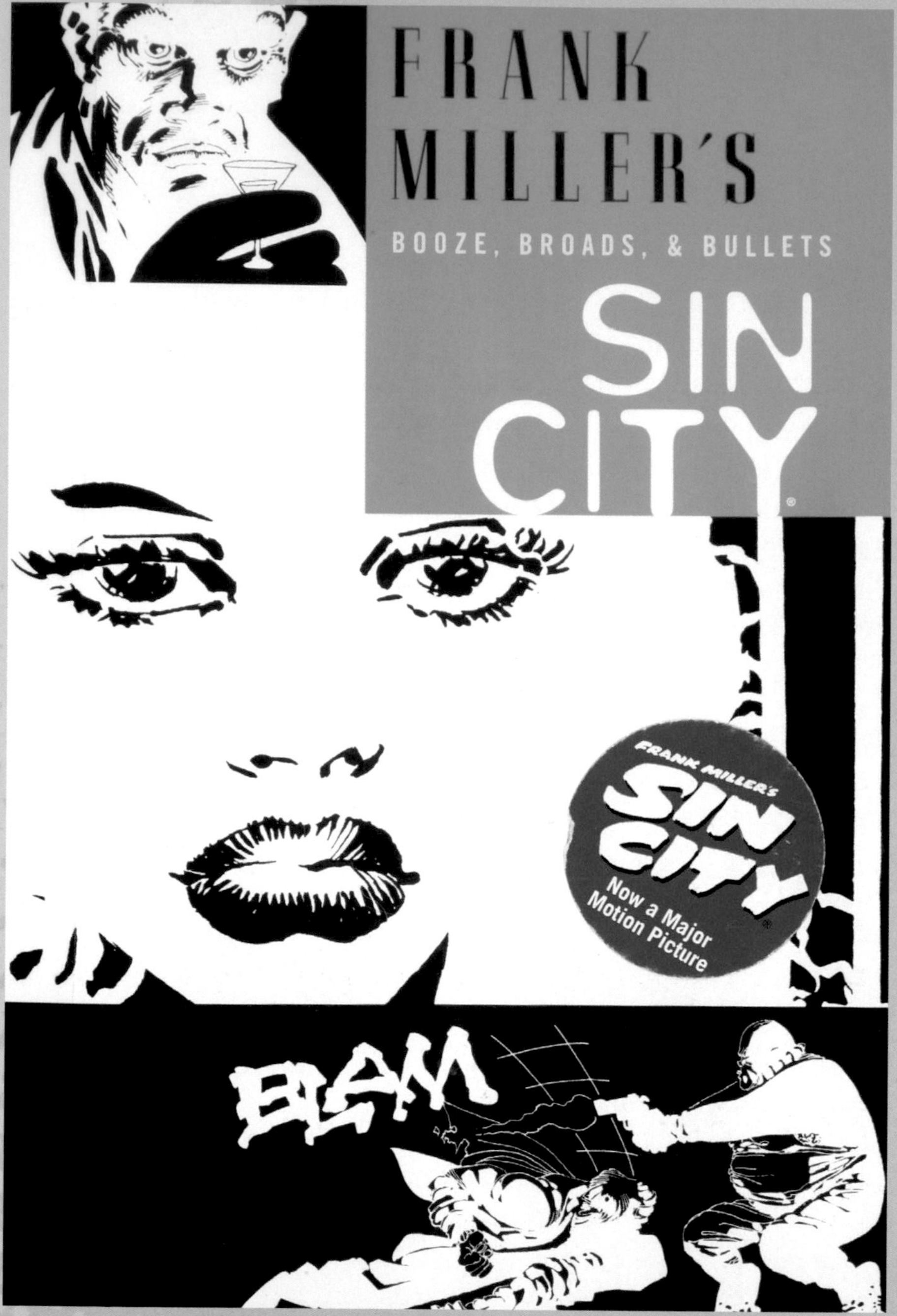
FRANK MILLER'S
BOOZE, BROADS, & BULLETS
SIN CITY
FRANK MILLER'S SIN CITY
Now a Major Motion Picture
BLAM

In Frank Miller's *Sin City*, Basin City police fight against a large underworld of criminal organizations and gangs.

worry about. There is no main character, but a recurring cast is regularly shot, stabbed, and maimed. The good news is that they never seem to die. The bad news is that they have to continue to live in Sin City.

Mainstream publishers followed these trends and added edgy characters and titles of their own. They also did not hesitate to revamp and reinvent existing characters. For example, Marvel, recovering from bankruptcy with new management, mutated the X-Men in the 1990s. The X-Men had always been multicultural, but with new direction, their international flavor grew considerably. Mutants lived the world over, and the X-Men focus expanded to include more of them. The New X-Men, as they were called, eventually split into two teams under the leadership of Professor X. Spin-offs featured teenage mutants and solo series for the characters who appeared to be the most popular.

These changes and others underscored the varied subjects and design that comic books were exploring as the twenty-first century began. But their continued success was not something to take for granted, and publishers are working to remain daring and innovative.

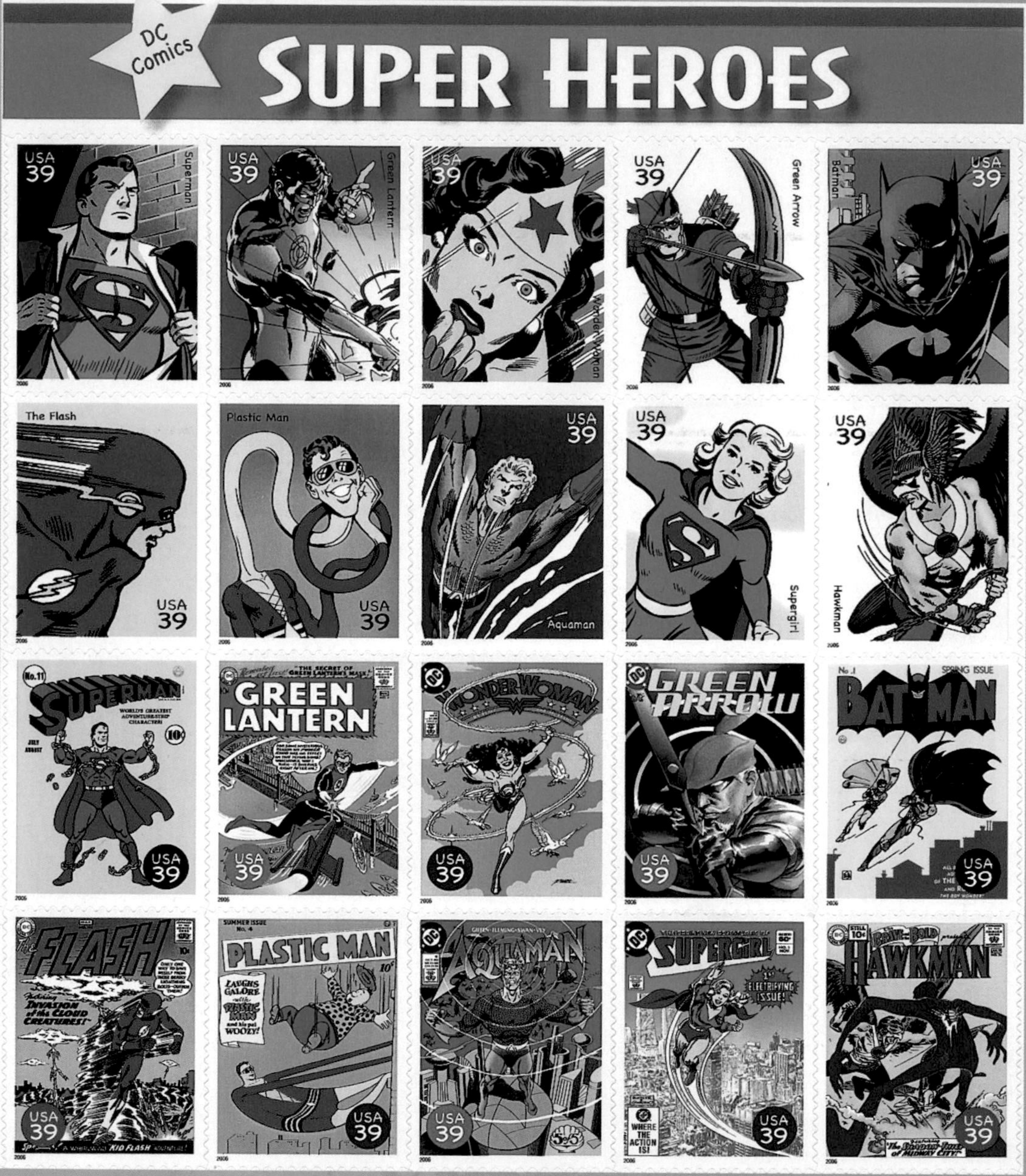
DC Comics
SUPER HEROES
USA 39
Superman
Green Lantern
Wonder Woman
Green Arrow
Batman
The Flash
Plastic Man
Aquaman
Supergirl
Hawkman
SUPERMAN
GREEN LANTERN
WONDER WOMAN
GREEN ARROW
BATMAN
FLASH
PLASTIC MAN
AQUAMAN
SUPERGIRL
HAWKMAN

In 2006 the United States Postal Service issued a series of postage stamps commemorating America's comic book superheroes.

EPILOGUE

The world of comics in the early twenty-first century has a freedom undreamed of a generation ago. Society and mainstream readers are open to all kinds of publications with plenty of room for sex and violence and other former taboos. For example, a long-standing Marvel cowboy hero, the Rawhide Kid, was revealed to be gay in a 2003 series. And in 2006, *The 9/11 Report,* a graphic novel by Sid Jacobson and Ernie Colón, recounted a sensitive event from recent history—the September 11, 2001, terrorist attacks on the United States. However, as each new barrier is breached, the ability to surprise readers with something truly new and different becomes harder. Comic books continue to search for new and edgier frontiers.

GRAPHIC CHANGES

A challenge to the traditional comic book is the continued power, growth, and interactivity of the Internet. Combined with the increasing sophistication of video games, the Internet erodes the base of traditional comic book readers while at the same time opening a new world of comic blogs and web comics. Another bright spot is the dramatic increase in sales of graphic novels in bookstores. The *Retailers Guide to Graphic Novels* expects that the graphic novel is, in fact, "poised to pass the traditional comic as the dominant form." Increasingly, graphic novels are gaining shelf space in mainstream

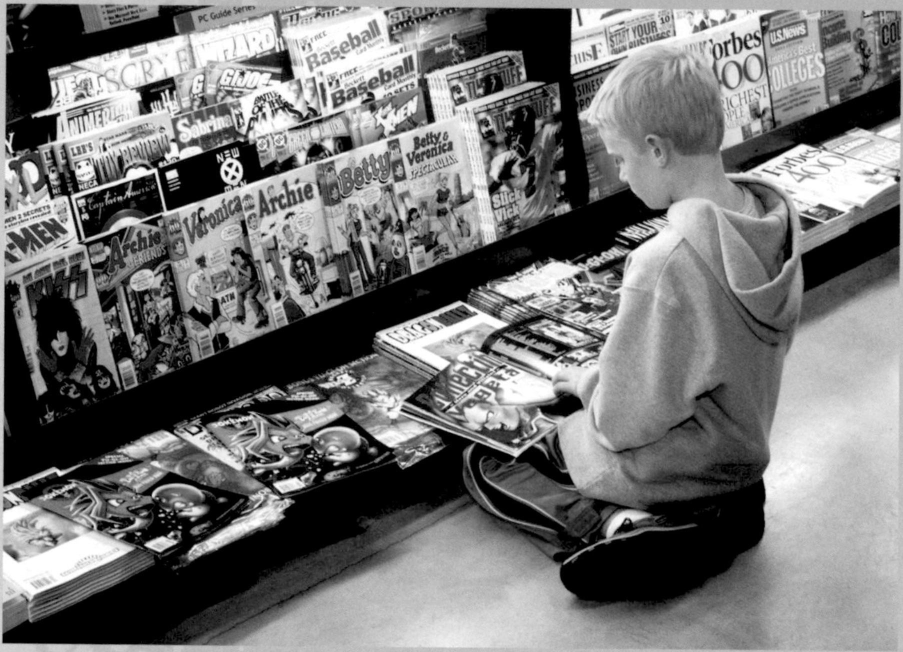
Baseball
Baseball
Sabrina
Archie
Veronica
Betty
Betty & Veronica
Forbes
400
U.S.News
X-MEN

A young boy looks at comic books in a large bookstore. In the late 1990s, many mainstream bookstores began developing special sections for comic books and graphic novels.

bookstores. They are also being reviewed (and gaining publicity) in influential book industry periodicals such as *Publisher's Weekly* and *School Library Journal*. Alison Bechdel's *Fun Home* was even on the *New York Times* nonfiction best-seller list in June 2006.

And in the early twenty-first century, major movie studios have released big-budget spin-offs of comics and graphic novels starring popular actors. The list is long and growing: *X-Men* (2000), *Spider-Man* (2002), *Daredevil* (2003), *The League of Extraordinary Gentlemen* (2003), *X-2* (2003), *Catwoman* (2004), *Hellboy* (2004), *Spider-Man 2* (2004), *Elektra* (2005), *Fantastic 4* (2005), *Sin City* (2005), *V for Vendetta* (2006), and *X-Men: The Last Stand* (2006). Interestingly, many of these movies' plots follow original or classic comic story lines rather than any later alterations. (One exception is *Batman*

Begins [2005], which adds a mystical Tibetan element to Batman's traditional background.)

While the news about graphic novels and film adaptations is encouraging, it comes at a price. Artist and writer Mike Kunkel fears that comic books have come too far from their beginnings, leaving young readers behind. "I think that there are too many creations out there that are not for kids at all," he says. "And that's fine for the industry to have a wide spectrum of bizarre and outrageous stuff, but we have to go the other way and offer a lot of variety in the all-ages category. Give kids something to start with and grow up on. . . . [M]aybe we've forgotten what it was like to be just starting out collecting comics and appreciating the innocence in stories."

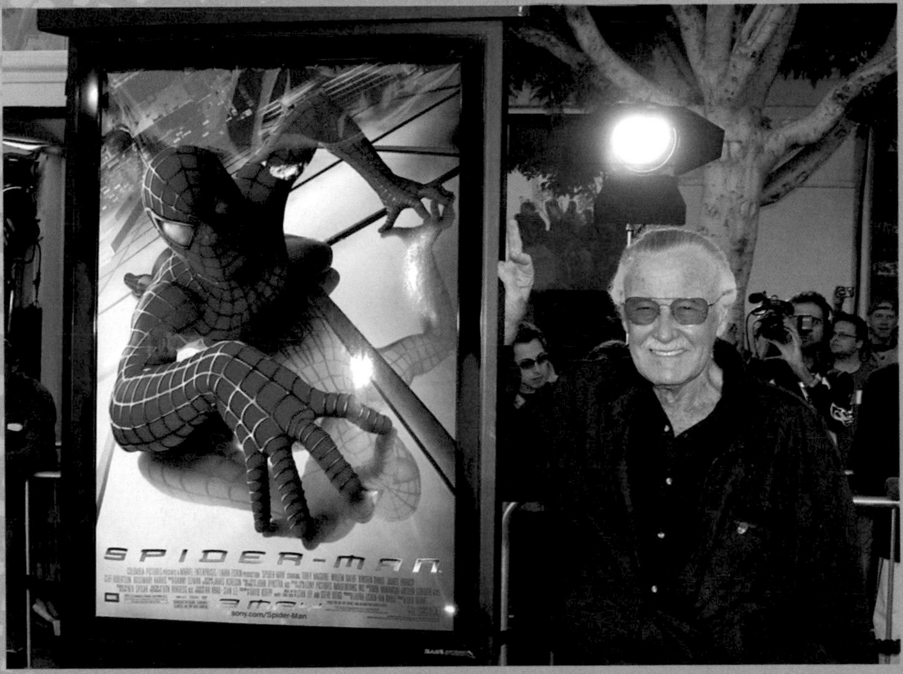
SPIDER-MAN

Stan Lee poses next to a poster of his comic book creation at the 2002 Los Angeles, California, premiere of the movie *Spider-Man*.

X-Men 2 (2003) stars Hugh Jackman as Wolverine *(left)* and Patrick Stewart as Professor X *(right)*.

A DIFFERENT WORLD

Are there new characters that can excite young readers the way Superman or Spider-Man excited their parents or grandparents a generation or two ago? Maybe. But will these types of characters continue to appear first on the printed page? That is harder to say.

Some comic book characters—Spider-Man and the X-Men, for example—have reached undreamed of popularity through the success of movies based on their characters. But that success does not necessarily translate into increased sales for printed comic books. Once you have watched Spider-Man digitally roaming across the New York skyline, seeing him do the same thing on a paneled page may seem pretty tame. The financial rewards of spin-offs also place pressure on mainstream comic book publishers. What kind of merchandising potential can the characters generate? Toys? Games? Action figures?

And if not, should the publisher bother bringing out the comic book at all?

This is the challenge facing American comic books in the 2000s. To the optimist, comics span a wider range of subjects and approaches than ever before. Yet that range does not translate into an ever-growing popularity. Once upon a time, comic books held a special place in the minds of children looking to escape the everyday world. The special mixture of art and words made the stories come alive in a way that words alone could not always match. And the subject matter, particularly involving superheroes, was not easily found anywhere else.

But young audiences in the twenty-first century face options that Jerry Siegel, Joe Shuster, Jack Kirby, Joe Simon, and Will Eisner never imagined early in their careers. Cable television, with its specialty networks such as Nickelodeon, the Cartoon Network, Comedy Central, or the SciFi Channel, absorb kids' time and attention. And interactive video games and the Internet have taken comics into a whole new realm. Brian Miller also points out the rising cost of comic books. "If a child has to choose between reading one comic book or renting a video for a week, what do you think the outcome will be?"

Comic books will survive because they are a unique and appealing art form. But whether they can continue to hold a prominent position in an increasingly fractured pop culture world remains to be seen.

Timeline

1929 The Great Depression begins.

1934 Max Gaines and Harry Wildenberg begin *Famous Funnies*. Major Malcolm Wheeler-Nicholson forms National Allied Publications to publish original comic books.

1938 Superman makes his first comic-book appearance in DC-National's *Action Comics*.

1939 World War II begins in Europe. Batman debuts in *Detective Comics*.

1940 Captain Marvel debuts in Fawcett Comics. Pressure for the United States to enter World War II grows after Germany bombs Great Britain. Will Eisner creates *The Spirit*.

1941 Jack Kirby and Joe Simon team up to create Captain America for Timely Comics. Wonder Woman first appears in *All Star Comics*. The United States enters World War II.

1945 World War II ends with an Allied victory. The baby boom, a huge increase in U.S. birthrates, begins. Tensions between the Soviet Union and its former allies in the West mark the start of the Cold War.

1953 Wisconsin senator Joseph McCarthy begins Senate hearings to investigate the so-called Communist threat to the United States.

1954 Frederic Wertham publishes *The Seduction of the Innocent*. Comic book publishers develop the Comics Code Authority.

1961 The United States sends soldiers into the Vietnam conflict. Stan Lee and Jack Kirby create the Fantastic Four.

1962 Lee and Kirby create the Hulk. Lee creates Spider-Man and Thor. Archie Comics spawns two spin-offs, *Sabrina the Teenaged Witch* and *Josie and the Pussycats*.

1966 Marvel Comics debuts its first African American superhero, the Black Panther.

1968 Robert Crumb begins publishing Zap Comix.

1970 Trina Robbins and Willy Mendes begin publishing underground feminist comix.

1978 Will Eisner publishes *A Contract with God*.

1984 Kevin Eastman and Peter Laird create *Teenage Mutant Ninja Turtles* #1.

1986 Frank Miller creates *Batman: The Dark Knight Returns* for DC. DC begins Alan Moore's *Watchmen*. Art Spiegelman publishes *Maus*.

1989 DC begins Neil Gaiman's *The Sandman*. The Berlin Wall in Germany is torn down, symbolizing the end of the Cold War.

1992 Spiegelman publishes *Maus II* and is awarded a special Pulitzer Prize.

1993 Superman is killed by Doomsday. DC resurrects Superman. Dark Horse Comics releases *Hellboy* and *Sin City*.

1996 Marvel Comics declares bankruptcy.

2000 A movie version of the *X-Men* is released.

2001 Terrorists attack the World Trade Center in New York City and the Pentagon near Washington, D.C.

2005 A movie version of Frank Miller's *Sin City* premieres. Christian Bale stars in the movie *Batman Begins*. Will Eisner dies in Florida.

2006 Sid Jacobson and Ernie Colón create the graphic novel *The 9/11 Report*. The movie *X-Men: The Last Stand* premieres.

Selected Famous Names in Comic Book History

Will Eisner (1917–2005) Eisner was born in Brooklyn, New York, the son of Jewish immigrants. He became interested in art in high school. After graduation, Eisner worked as a writer and artist on newspaper comic strips. In 1939 he created the Spirit, one of his most enduring characters. In the 1970s, Eisner focused on developing the comic book format to tell more complex stories. This led to the 1978 publication of *A Contract with God*, four short stories set in a depression-era tenement. Eisner called *A Contract with God* a graphic novel, and since then, the term has come into common use. In his later years, Eisner taught at the School of Visual Arts in New York City and wrote books about graphic storytelling.

Neil Gaiman (b. 1960) Born in Portchester, England, Gaiman grew up reading science fiction and fantasy novels. He began his career as a journalist but became interested in comic book writing after befriending Alan Moore, the author of *V for Vendetta* and *Watchmen*. In the 1980s, Gaiman began writing his own series for DC Comics. In 1988 DC published the first issue of Gaiman's *The Sandman*. *The Sandman* used elements of mythology, fantasy and horror literature, history, and religion. Gaiman has also written award-winning short stories, novels, children's books, television scripts, and screenplays. He has lived in the United States since the 1990s.

Stan Lee (b. 1922) Born Stanley Lieber in New York City, Stan Lee was one of the driving forces behind the growth of Marvel Comics. After high school, Lee was hired as an assistant at Timely Comics. At nineteen he was promoted to editor, then to art director. Lee wrote in many genres for Timely (later renamed Marvel Comics), but in the 1950s, he focused on superheroes. Working with artists Jack Kirby and Steve Ditko, Lee created the Fantastic Four, the Incredible Hulk, Thor, the X-Men, Spider-Man, and others. Lee is a popular fixture at comic-book industry and movie events.

Frank Miller (b. 1957) Writer and artist Miller grew up in Vermont. His childhood love of comic books sparked an interest in art. In the late 1970s, Miller was hired as a penciller for DC Comics and Marvel. Miller began introducing elements of Japanese manga (not well-known in the United States then) into his art. In 1986 Miller wrote and drew *Batman: The Dark Knight Returns*, an atmospheric and sophisticated version of the series. Miller carried his film noir style into *Sin City,* a Dark Horse Comics serial begun in 1991.

Trina Robbins (b. 1938) Writer and artist Robbins left New York in 1970 to join San Francisco's underground comix scene. Robbins helped create the feminist publications *It Ain't Me, Babe* and *Wimmen's Comix*, which provided outlets for women writers and artists. With artist Anne Timmons, Robbins created the on-going series *Go Girl!* in 2000. She has also written several books on the history of women in the comic book industry, including *A Century of Women Cartoonists, The Great Women Superheroes,* and *From Girls to Grrlz.*

Art Spiegelman (b. 1948) Born in Sweden, Spiegelman came to the United States with his parents, both survivors of Nazi concentration camps. Spiegelman's parents wanted him to become a dentist, but he had his mind set on cartooning. After college, Spiegelman joined the underground comix movement. In 1972 Spiegelman created mouse characters that represented Jews living in Nazi-occupied Poland, relying on his father's personal memories for story lines. Deciding to turn the stories into a full-length graphic novel, Spiegelman created *Maus*, published in 1986. *Maus II: And Here My Troubles Began* followed in 1991. Spiegelman was awarded a special Pulitzer Prize in 1992. A New York resident, Spiegelman lived only blocks from the World Trade Center when it was attacked by terrorists in September 2001. In 2004 he expressed his experience of the attack in a comic book Sunday supplement, *In the Shadow of No Towers.*

Source Notes

6 Bradford W. Wright, *Comic Book Nation: The Transformation of Youth Culture in America* (Baltimore: Johns Hopkins University Press, 2001), xiii.

15 Jerry Siegel, *Action Comics* #1, illustrated by Joe Shuster (New York: Detective Comics, 1938).

17 Jerry Siegel, "In the Beginning," 1983, http://theages.superman .ws/superman.php (September 29, 2006).

18 Ibid.

18 Ibid.

19–20 Daniele Di Piazza, email interview with author, August 9, 2006.

20–21 Bob Kane, quoted in Sarah Boxer, "Bob Kane, 83, the Cartoonist Who Created 'Batman,' Is Dead," *New York Times*, November 7, 1998, http://www.nytimes.com/learning/ general/onthisday/bday/1024.html (September 29, 2006).

21–22 Bob Kane, *Detective Comics* #27 (New York: Detective Comics, 1939).

22 Ibid.

25 Stanley Lieber (Stan Lee), *Mystic Comics* #6, illustrated by Alex Schomburg (New York: Timely Comics, 1941).

27 Sterling North, *Chicago Daily News* editorial, May 8, 1940, quoted in Ron Goulart, *Great American Comic Books* (Portland, OR: Collectors Press, 2000), 200.

28 Joe Simon, quoted in Les Daniels, *Marvel: Five Decades of the World's Greatest Comics* (New York: Harry N. Abrams, 1991), 40.

33 Matthew J. Pustz, *Comic Book Culture: Fanboys and True Believers* (Jackson: University of Mississippi Press, 1999), 29.

35 *Comic Book Section*, June 1940, quoted in *Wildwood Cemetery: The Spirit Database*, http://www .angelfire.com/art/wildwood (August 15, 2006).

40–41 Will Eisner, quoted in Jules Feiffer, *The Great Comic Book Heroes* (New York: Bonanza Books, 1965), 33.

42–43 Feiffer, *The Great Comic Book Heroes*, 15.

43 Bill Hauser, email interview with author, August 24, 2006.

45 Comics Code Authority of 1954, quoted in *Comicartville Library*, n.d., http://www.comicartville.com/ comicscode.htm (September 29, 2006).

48 Frederic Wertham, quoted in Marc Singer, "'Black Skins' and White Masks: Comic Books and the Secret of Race," *African American Review* 36, no. 1 (2002), 107–120.

48–49 Frederic Wertham, *The Seduction of the Innocent* (New York: Rinehart & Co., 1954), 10.

50 Goulart, *Great American Comic Books*, 216.

51 Comics Code Authority of 1954, quoted in *Comicartville Library*.

52 Goulart, Ron. *Great American Comic Books*, 216.

55 Stan Lee, *The Fantastic Four* #1, illustrated by Jack Kirby (New York: Marvel Comics, 1961).

56 Kenneth Plume "Interview with Stan Lee," *FilmForce.IGN.com*, June 26, 2000, http://movies.ign.com/ articles/035/035881p1.html (September 29, 2006).

56–57 Gerard Jones and Will Jacobs, *The Comic Book Heroes: The First History of Modern Comic Books from the Silver Age to the Present* (Rocklin, CA: Prima Publishing, 1997), 50.

58 Plume, "Interview with Stan Lee."

58 Ibid.

61 Ibid.

61 Ibid.

65 Jeff Limke, email interview with author, August 2, 2006.

65–66 Mary Rodgers, email interview with author, August 2, 2006.

69 Robert Crumb, poster (San Francisco: Zap Comix, 1968).

77 Will Eisner, keynote address (Will Eisner Symposium, Department of English, University of Florida, Gainesville, February 20–21, 2002). Available online at *ImageText: Interdisciplinary Comics Studies 1.1* (2004), http://www.english.ufl.edu/imagetext/archives/v1_1/eisner/index.shtml (August 7, 2006).

79 "Radioactive Man," episode 2F17 (September 24, 1995), *The Simpsons*, written by John Swartzwelder. Quoted in *The Simpsons Archive*, n.d., http://www.snpp.com/episodes/2F17.html (September 29, 2006).

81 Brian Miller, email interview with author, September 11, 2006.

84 Rafael Pi Roman, "Healing Images," *York Voices*, n.d., http://www.thirteen.org/nyvoices/features/healingimage.html (September 29, 2006).

84–85 Justine Fontes, email interview with author, September 2, 2006.

87 Pustz, *Comic Book Culture*, 19.

87–88 Les Daniels, *DC Comics: A Celebration of the World's Favorite Comic Book Heroes*, (New York: Watson-Guptill Publications, 2003), 218.

95 Danny Fingeroth, *Superman on the Couch* (New York: Continuum, 2004), 14.

95 *ICv2: Retailers Guide to Graphic Novels #7*, Q2 (2006): 4.

97 Mike Kunkel, quoted in "Quote of the Week," n.d., http://albert.nickerson.tripod.com/quotes.html (September 29, 2006).

99 Miller, email interview.

Selected Bibliography

Berger, Arthur Asa. *The Comic-Stripped American*. New York: Walker Publishing Company, 1973.

Daniels, Les. *DC Comics: A Celebration of the World's Favorite Comic Book Heroes*. New York: Watson-Guptill Publications, 2003.

————— *Marvel: Five Decades of the World's Greatest Comics*. New York: Harry N. Abrams, 1991.

Feiffer, Jules. *The Great Comic Book Heroes*. New York: Bonanza Books, 1965.

Fingeroth, Danny. *Superman on the Couch*. Foreword by Stan Lee. New York: Continuum, 2004.

Goulart, Ron. *Comic Book Culture: An Illustrated History*. Portland, OR: Collectors Press, 2000.

Jones, Gerard, and Will Jacobs. *The Comic Book Heroes: The First History of Modern Comic Books from the Silver Age to the Present*. Rocklin, CA: Prima Publishing, 1997.

McCloud, Scott. *Understanding Comics*. Princeton, WI: Kitchen Sink Press, 1993. Reprint, New York: Harper Collins, 1994.

Pellowski, Michael Morgan. *The Art of Making Comic Books*. Minneapolis: Lerner Publications Company, 1995.

Pustz, Matthew J. *Comic Book Culture: Fanboys and True Believers*. Jackson: University of Mississippi Press, 1999.

Simon, Joe, with Jim Simon. *The Comic Book Makers*. New York: Crestwood/II Publications, 1990.

Wertham, Frederic. *The Seduction of the Innocent*. New York: Rinehart & Co., 1954.

Wright, Bradford W. *Comic Book Nation: The Transformation of Youth Culture in America*. Baltimore: Johns Hopkins University Press, 2001.

Further Reading and Websites

Books

Coleman, Jerry et al. *Superman*. Vol. 1. New York: DC Comics, 2005. This is a collection of Superman comics from 1959 to 1963, when he faced some of his most memorable villains including Brainiac and learned that he had a surviving cousin from Krypton who became Supergirl.

Conroy, Mike. *500 Comic Book Villains*. Hauppauge, NY: Barron's, 2004. Conroy gives readers the lowdown on every major bad guy who ever made mischief, caused trouble, or took a shot at world domination.

Dougall, Alastair, ed. *The DC Comics Encyclopedia*. New York: DK Publishing, 2004. This comprehensive and fully illustrated reference book identifies and explains the context for all of the DC characters.

Goulart, Ron. *Great American Comic Books*. Lincolnwood, IL: Publications International, 2001. This in-depth look at American comic books traces their development and evolution over the past century.

Graphic Myths and Legends Series. Minneapolis: Graphic Universe, 2007. The Graphic Myths and Legends series uses the graphic novel format to bring classic stories to life for young readers. Titles include *Amaterasu: Return of the Sun; Hercules: The Twelve Labors; Isis & Osiris: To the Ends of the Earth; King Arthur: Excalibur Unsheathed; Thor & Loki: In the Land of Giants;* and *Yu the Great: Conquering the Flood,* among others.

Lee, Stan, Steve Ditko, et al. *Stan Lee Presents the Amazing Spider-Man*. Vol. 1. New York: Marvel Comics, 2002. This compilation of Spider-Man's first exploits includes his original story and many of his early adventures.

Miller, Frank. *The Dark Knight Returns*. New York: DC Comics, 1996. Miller reinvents and reinvigorates the traditional Batman story with a darker edge. An older Batman, seemingly retired for ten years, returns to a nightmarish Gotham City to challenge evil once again.

Moore, Alan. *Watchmen*. New York: Warner Books, 1987. Old super-heroes, whose lives are ordinary at best, are being killed off as nuclear war threatens the world.

Sabin, Roger. *Comics, Comix & Graphic Novels: A History of Comic Art*. London: Phaidon Press, 1996. This extensively illustrated history covers everything from the eighteenth- and nineteenth-century work that inspired the first comics to the artistic innovations of the twentieth century.

Sanderson, Peter. *Marvel Universe*. New York: Harry N. Abrams, 1996. The Marvel universe of characters is a big place, and it has to fit in everyone from the Incredible Hulk to Galactus, the Devourer of Worlds. But this one book manages to include them all, whether they get along or not.

Satrapi, Marjane. *Persepolis: The Story of a Childhood*. New York: Pantheon, 2004. Satrapi tells her autobiographical story of growing up in Iran during the Iranian Revolution of 1979 and during the Iran-Iraq War of the 1980s.

Spiegelman, Art. *Maus: A Survivor's Tale*. New York: Pantheon Books, 1987. Spiegelman tells the story of his father's imprisonment during World War II from a cartoon perspective. *Maus II: And Here My Troubles Began* (New York: Pantheon Books, 1992) continues the story, detailing how the family is haunted by memories of the prison camp long after the war ends.

Websites

Archie Comics. http://www.archiecomics.com. The Archie Comics headquarters features news, trivia and jokes, downloadable computer wallpaper, an interactive map of Riverdale, and past issues of *Archie* and its spinoffs.

The Collector Times. http://www.collectortimes.com. This site traces the history of comic books from their nineteenth-century origins to the mid-1990s. It includes an art gallery and articles on collectibles, gaming, and comics collecting.

Comics Research.org. http://www.comicsresearch.org. This scholarly site directs visitors to books, articles, and other resources on a wide variety of comic book subjects.

DC Comics. http://www.dccomics.com. DC's website features the latest information on the company's mainstream, manga, Vertigo, and Wildstorm lines. Readers can get sneak peeks at upcoming issues, read interviews with writers and artists, and download mini-posters and screen savers.

Marvel Comics. http://www.marvel.com/comics. Marvel's site is headquarters for all the latest news on Marvel comic books and movie connections. A searchable encyclopedia details the characters and events in the Marvel Universe.

Toonopedia. http://www.toonopedia.com. Don Markstein's alphabetically organized reference site provides short articles on hundreds of comic book characters, past and present.

Will Eisner. http://www.willeisner.com. This site celebrates the work of Will Eisner, one of the few comic book creators to make an impact both at the beginning of the comic book era in the 1930s and as an innovator in the development of the graphic novel in the 1970s.

Index

Photo Acknowledgements

The images in this book are used with the permission of: Library of Congress, pp. 6 (LC-DIG-ppmsca-03291), 12 (LC-USZC4-2940), 30 (LC-USZC4-5602), 43 (LC-USZ62-126485); © CORBIS, p. 7; © 1944 Edgar Rice Burroughs, Inc., p. 8; © Eastern Color Printing Co., p. 9; Comics on Parade, © United Feature Syndicate, Inc., p. 11; © DC Comics, Inc., pp. 14, 18, 21, 32, 88; © Getty Images, pp. 16, 44, 71; © Bettmann/CORBIS, p. 22; © 2007 Marvel Characters, Inc. Used with permission, pp. 24, 57; © Fawcett Publications, Inc., p. 26; © DC Comics, Inc. Image provided by Getty Images, p. 29; © Thomas D. Mcavoy/Time Life Pictures/Getty Images, p. 33; The Spirit is © by and a registered trademark ® of Will Eisner Studios, Inc., pp. 34, 41; © Centaur Publications, Inc., p. 36; JUDGE HARDY & SON © RKO Pictures, Inc. Licensed by Warner Bros. Entertainment, Inc. All Rights Reserved. Image provided by © Underwood & Underwood/CORBIS, p. 37; © Archie Comics Publications, Inc., pp. 38, 66; © Okefenokee Glee & Perloo, Inc. Used by permission, p. 39; © SuperStock Inc./SuperStock, p. 46; AP Images, p. 49; © EC Comics, p. 50; © American Comics Group, Image provided by SuperStock, p. 53; © 2005 Marvel/CORBIS, pp. 54, 59, 60, 63, 64, 75, 90; © 2007 Marvel Characters, Inc. Used with permission. Image provided by Getty Images, p. 62; © Robert Crumb, (1968), p. 68; © Robert Crumb, (1968), Image provided by Getty Images, p. 73; © Brian Hamill/Getty Images, p. 76; "THE SIMPSONS"™ & © 1990 Twentieth Century Fox Television. All rights reserved, p. 78; © Todd Strand/Independent Picture Service, p. 80; "Teenage Mutant Ninja Turtles" copyright and trademark of Mirage Studios, Inc., p. 82; "Book Cover," from MAUS I: A SURVIVOR'S TALE/MY FATHER BLEEDS HISTORY by Art Spiegelman, copyright © 1973, 1981, 1982, 1984, 1985, 1986 by Art Spiegelman. Used by permission of Pantheon Books, a division of Random House, Inc., p. 85; © Virgo Productions/zefa/CORBIS, p. 86; "Sin City: Booze, Broads, & Bullets" © 1998, 2007 Frank Miller, Inc. All Rights Reserved. Sin City and the Sin City logo are registered trademarks of Frank Miller, Inc. Published by Dark Horse Comics, Inc., p. 92; Copyrighted stamp design of the United States Postal Service, p. 94; © age fotostock/SuperStock, p. 96; © Tammie Arroyo/Retna Ltd., p. 97; "X2" © 2003 Twentieth Century Fox. All rights reserved. Image courtesy of Everett Collection, p. 98.

Front Cover: © Dynamic Publications, Inc.

Titles from the award-winning People's History series:

For more information, please call 1-800-328-4929 or visit www.lernerbooks.com